An
Outline
of
Russian
Literature

by
Marc Slonim

 A MENTOR BOOK

Published by THE NEW AMERICAN LIBRARY

Published as a MENTOR BOOK
By Arrangement with Oxford University Press, Inc.

FIRST PRINTING, SEPTEMBER, 1959

MENTOR BOOKS are published by
The New American Library of World Literature, Inc.
501 Madison Avenue, New York 22, New York

PRINTED IN THE UNITED STATES OF AMERICA

THE RUSSIAN MIND

In this brilliant and stimulating survey of Russian literature, Marc Slonim traces its development from the religious manuscripts and folk epics of the Middle Ages down to the writings of such contemporary authors as Sholokhov and Pasternak.

With understanding, authority and insight, the noted critic and scholar discusses the work of the great poets, playwrights and novelists of the past ten centuries. He analyzes the specific qualities that set Russian literary schools apart from their European counterparts and he studies the influence that the important literary critics—Belinsky, Herzen, Chernyshevsky, Pisarev—had on Russian political and intellectual life.

Mr. Slonim surveys the literature of modern Russia —from the bright period of Soviet letters following the Revolution to the subsequent decline in the quality of Soviet fiction under the party state. He examines Russia's policy toward writers today and probes the possibility of a renaissance of literature in the Russia of the future.

THIS IS A REPRINT OF THE ORIGINAL HARDCOVER EDITION PUBLISHED BY OXFORD UNIVERSITY PRESS.

Other Books of Interest

And Quiet Flows the Don *by Mikhail Sholokhov*

An undisputed masterpiece about the vigorous, violent lives of the Don Cossacks of the early 1900's.
(#T1661—75¢)

The Brothers Karamazov *by Fyodor Dostoyevsky*

Complete and unabridged, the great classic about a passionate and tragic Russian family.
(#T1488—75¢)

Safe Conduct *by Boris Pasternak*

The brilliant autobiography, short stories and poems of one of the greatest writers of our time.
(#D1669—50¢)

Russia (revised) *by Bernard Pares*

An authoritative study of the background of the most controversial country in the world today.
(#MD230—50¢)

CONTENTS

1. THE ORIGINS

RUSSIAN literature did not make its appearance in the Western world until the second half of the nineteenth century, when Europe and America first heard of Turgenev, Tolstoy, Dostoevsky, and Gogol. As some French critics put it, it looked like an invasion. It also came as a surprise. Many were astounded by the fact that such a crop of writers, later joined by Chekhov, Gorky, Bunin, and others, suddenly emerged from the arctic darkness of Russian despotism and barbarity. The latest newcomer into the Republic of Letters, Russian literature seemed a phenomenon of spontaneous generation, with parents and ancestry unknown.

Of course, this fable of miraculous birth was mainly due to ignorance of Russia in general, and of literary history in particular. Russian writers had, like others, their deep roots, and could easily trace their literary genealogy. However, Russia's cultural development remained an isolated process. Despite its size, this huge land which stretched in Europe from the Carpathian Mountains to the Urals, and in Asia from the Urals to the Pacific, formed a continent apart and had but tenuous connexions with the West of the Middle Ages and the Renaissance. And there were other internal factors which determined the special character of Russian civilization until the eighteenth century, preventing the arts in Russia from developing as easily as in more fortunate countries.

It is common knowledge that the beginnings of Russian literature coincide with the introduction of Christianity into the state of Kiev at the end of the tenth century. The new faith was forced by the princes of Kiev upon their subjects to supplant the animism and paganism of the ancient Slavs. It came from Byzantium in the form of Eastern orthodoxy, and this was a fact of primary importance. While the rest of Europe got the Gospel from Rome and came of age within the forms and dogmas of the Roman Catholic Church and the Papacy, Russia received the light from the Constantinople, followed the Byzantine tradition and remained under the rule of the Greek Orthodox denomination—the latter, as is well known, did not recognize the authority of the Pope, whom it called 'the Bishop of Rome,' rejected the celibacy of the clergy, supported the use of national languages instead of Latin in liturgy, and, on top of various theological differences in the concepts of the Trinity, the Holy Ghost, and Communion, affirmed the unity of spiritual and secular power in the community of Christians.

Byzantine influence for five centuries defined the course of Russian culture and brought beneficial as well as harmful elements into Russian life. Byzantium was formal, rigid, and exclusive. It sustained its political despotism by a pompous and often corrupt hierarchy, it combined ascetic intransigence with lust and cruelty, it indulged in sectarian hair-splitting and in malicious scheming. Yet, at the same time, Byzantium posessed a fervour in Christian belief and a philosophical depth in its mysticism, and lived and acted as the direct heir of the Hellenic-Roman civilization. The traditions of Athens and Alexandria were preserved in Constantinople. Byzantine missionaries, priests, scholars, and artists transmitted to Russia some of the spirit of the philosophers and poets of the ancient world. The alphabet of the early Russian Church was taken from the Greek. The first literary works were translated from the same language (as well as from Bulgarian), and the clerics who laid down the foundations of the written language came from Constantinople or had been trained in other Byzantine centres of learning.

In the tenth and eleventh centuries written literature served the needs of the Church and was promoted mainly by priests and monks. One of the first books to appear in Russia was the eleventh-century copy of the New Testament made for Ostromir, ruler of the northern city of Novgorod. Sermons, lives of saints, prophetic revelations, apocrypha, legends and myths lacking the official approval of the Church, and pateriki, or anthologies of moralistic maxims and semi-religious anecdotes, all followed suit. Between the eleventh and fourteenth centuries, the overwhelming majority of manuscripts (688 out of 708), including travelogues like the *Pilgrimage to the Holy Land* by Daniil, were of clerical content, written in Church Slavonic and preserving the traditions of Greek rhetoric and the figurative style of the Bible. As a whole, this literature was moralistic and its object was to instruct and guide. Princes and bishops looked upon it as a good educational foundation, and Church Slavonic became identified with the literary expression of divine or lofty matters. Thus, from its inception, Russian literature had a religious, didactic, and practical (in so far as social) aim. This fundamental emphasis on moral and social usefulness has remained to this day.

The literary language of the Church, however, was confined to a restricted group of ecclesiastic and political rulers, whereas the common people used the colloquial language of daily life. Church Slavonic bore the heavy imprint of its foreign origin, and often sounded excessively pompous and scholarly; and only the educated few could write it. Long before its introduction, the Slavs of the Kievan State, or of the northern towns of Novgorod and Pskov and all along the great rivers of Pechora, Dnieper, Volga, and Don, told tales and sang songs in their own tongue. This spoken language continued to develop independently of Church Slavonic, or under its influence when subject matter demanded an ornate 'high' style. A whole series of profane works made their appearance in this idiomatic Russian. Some of them remained within the educational tradition: *The Russian Truth* by Yaroslav the Wise, prince of Kiev (eleventh century), or *Testament* by Vladimir Monomachos (twelfth century) are addressed to heirs and heads of families, and instruct them how to organize households and how to administer kingdoms. Even the most important historical works of the Middle Ages, *The Chronicles,* have a didactic flavour. The most important of them, usually called the *First Russian Chronicle,* is attributed to the friar Nestor (1120), who probably had assembled and edited the writings of various predecessors and had utilized different Greek materials. Written in a lively style, remarkable in its simplicity and dramatic power, it forms a bridge between moralistic works and those legends and books of travel which took the place of fiction in the twelfth and thirteen centuries.

Although religious and historical works were permeated by the Christian spirit, the pagan tradition was preserved in the folklore. Naïve and cunning fairy tales, epic and love songs, riddles, proverbs, and spells formed a rich treasury of oral poetry which expressed the fantasy and emotions of the people, mostly peasants and warriors. Even the spread of the Christian religion could not erase animistic concepts, mythological images, or ancient ritualistic patterns in Russian folklore. The vitality of these pagan elements is shown by their survival in the oral tradition up to our times.

Next to fairy tales in which firebirds are caught by young peasants, simpletons become princes, truth wrestles with injustice, and maidens ride grey wolves, the most important remnants of ancient folklore are folk chants or *byliny,* epic songs about Men of Might, some of which are not unlike the ballads of the King Arthur cycle. They probably came into being between the eighth and the tenth century, when the Russians along the Dnieper and the rivers of the North were passing from tribal to feudal organization, and when Kiev and Novgorod emerged as the main centres of the country. Even in later variants one can easily trace the different geographical birth places of *byliny.* They followed local traditions, but in general were developed from war songs passed on to the people by court minstrels. It is reasonable to assume that many of these *byliny* reflected at first such important events of national life as the struggle against the Asiatic raiders, the Polovetz, Pechenegues, and Tartars, the fight between rival princes, the trade relations of Novgorod with its Western neighbours, or the colonization of Russia by bold groups of pioneers who went up the main rivers and explored the wilderness of endless forests. But gradually historical reality was either obscured or sublimated by generations of popular reciters. Regional songs, mythological reminiscences, symbolic images, political allusions, and literary influences—both native and foreign—enriched and changed the whole body of these epic songs. Their heroes became detached symbols, and they embodied national characteristics. Ilya Murometz, the powerful giant who receives, like Antaeus, all his strength from contact with the earth, represents the ideal of might and patriotism; Mikula Selianinovich is obviously a champion of peasant virtues; Alesha Popovich is the epitome of youthful daring; and Sadko, the Rich Guest, of commercial initiative. Poetically the *byliny,* with their rhythmic recitative and animistic metaphors, are remarkable specimens of the epic genre and a source of inspiration for thousands of Russian poets and musicians (the opera *Sadko* by Rimsky-Korsakov, *Dobrynia Nikitich* by A. Grechaninov, and *Men of Might* by A. Borodin, are typical descendants of *byliny* in Russian music).

The folklore, on the one hand with its pagan spirit and the imaginative style of the popular spoken language, and on the other the religious and scholarly manner of the written Church Slavonic, represented the main body of Russian literature in the Middle Ages; but in the twelfth and thirteenth centuries there were also indications of the quest for new and independent poetic forms. Various songs belonged neither to folklore nor to Church Slavonic traditions, and the greatest work of the period, *The Lay of Igor,* composed probably at the end of the twelfth or at the beginning of the thirteenth century, stands apart as an original achievement, comparable only to the *Song of Roland.* The theme of this moving epic is the defeat of Prince Igor in his struggle against the Polovetz, the Asiatic invaders, and his capture by his foes. The author of the Lay possessed a keen sense of nature and a highly developed national consciousness. His descriptions of events are vivid and dramatic, and his lyrical passages, relating for example the grief of Igor's wife, are emotionally poignant and poetically fresh. The formal unity and the poetic perfection of this Lay place it above all the other work of the period. It testifies that by the thirteenth century Russian poetry had reached a high level of achievement and could be favourably compared with its European counterparts. It was the period when Kiev as well as the cities of Central and Northern Russia—Rostov, Suzdal, Novgorod, Pskov—set high standards in architecture, painting (mostly the art of the Ikon, the holy image), and statesmanship.

The normal development of Russian culture was, however, interrupted by wars and foreign occupation. The avalanche of Asiatic invasions destroyed the Kievan state, and the Slavic princes failed in their attempts to stop the Tartar hordes. By 1240 the whole of Russia was definitely conquered by the Mongols, and their rule lasted for over two centuries (until 1480). During this period, Russia, divided into small principalities with a social and economic structure similar to European feudalism, was a part of the vast Mongolian Empire of Genghis Khan, Tamerlane, and their successors. Even though some modern historians question whether living within the Asiatic orbit was wholly unfruitful for the Russians, there is no doubt that the Tartar domination, or the Tartar yoke, as the Russian people called it, had thwarted the organic growth of the land, isolated it from Western civilization, and was responsible in general for its cultural and material backwardness. Russian twentieth-century writers such as Gorky firmly believed that cruelty, physical violence, autocratic methods of administration, the subjugation of women, and all sorts of barbaric customs and manners came into Russian life with the Asiatic invaders.

The struggle against the Tartars and the efforts to unify the country, in which the rising principality of Moscow played such an important role during the fourteenth and fifteenth centuries, absorbed all the energies of the people. Literary works were few and of secondary value. But towards the end of the fifteenth century, a new political centre emerged. Moscow became a powerful state and a leader in the successful war against the Tartars. In the meantime, Constantinople succumbed to the Turks, and after its fall the rulers of Moscow called themselves czars (Caesars), heirs of the crumbled Byzantine Empire. Ivan III married Princess Sophia, descendant of the Paleologues. The collapse of Byzantium and the dismemberment of the Mongolian Empire left a gap in the East, and Moscow hurried to take over this heritage. The rise of Moscow gave a new impetus to the arts. Ties with the West were resumed. Italian architects were summoned to Moscow, and helped to build the Kremlin. The Russian school of painting blossomed with the masterpieces of the great Rublev, and secular as well as religious books increased in number and improved in quality. The sixteenth century left numerous works of prose, including political writings such as the opus by the abbott Philothei, who formulated the theory of Russian nationalism—he claimed that after the fall of Rome and Byzantium, Moscow was elected by the Almighty to become the see of a great Empire and guardian of the true Christian faith. 'Moscow is the third Rome,' he stated, 'and there will be no fourth.'

The first printed book, *The Apostle,* came off the press in 1564. Lives of saints, and various religious and moralistic works followed, and from Moscow printing plants spread to all Russian cities. Writers such as Ivan Peresvetov, author of a book of travels, and Maxim the Greek, an eloquent defender of Christian orthodoxy, are the most prominent literary figures of the period—together with the czar Ivan the Terrible, whose correspondence with Prince Kurbsky, his former friend and later a political exile associated with the Poles, is one of the most colourful and passionate documents of both Russian history and literature. It reflected the era of ruthless wars, the rivalry of princelings, and the ferocious taming of the old artistocracy by the power-hungry czarist rulers.

After Ivan's death in 1584, Russia went through tragic years of civil strife and foreign intervention. The throne of Moscow passed from legal heirs to pretenders and adventurers; assassination and rebellion replaced the law of succession; Poles and Swedes invaded the country; and Russia seemed on the brink of total disintegration. An alliance of common people with patriotic noblemen, however, brought about the restoration of order, and after a quarter of a century of troubles Mikhail Romanov was elected Czar by the National Assembly (Zemsky Sobor). He began the Romanov dynasty, and under him the country could return to peaceful tasks.

One of the most salient events of the seventeenth century was the revision of liturgical books, which contained many errors made by translators and copyists, and the subsequent reform of Church ritual. This Russian reformation led to a schism: the supporters of new measures, backed by the Czar and Church dignitaries, formed the faithful flock of the official Greek Orthodox denomination, while the Old Believers, or Schismatics, stubbornly clung to ancient books and ritual, refused to make the sign of the cross with three fingers (after the Greek usage) instead of the old two, and vituperated the bishops who obeyed their superiors. The Old Believers were persecuted by both ecclesiastical and secular authorities; and in order to escape imprisonment and torture they migrated to Siberia, to the Caucasus, and to the borderlands of Russia. Later they were broken down into a number of sects but all of them preserved for centuries their beliefs and puritanical customs. Many nineteenth- and twentieth-century Russian writers, from Melnikov and Leskov to Gorky, attracted by the originality of the Old

Believers, depicted their way of life, which followed ancient patterns of righteousness and strict religious zeal.

One of the martyrs of the Old Believers, Archpresbyter Avvakum, who was burned at the stake in 1682, was also a most remarkable writer. His *Life,* or autobiography, pathetic, racy, and witty, is written in the spoken tongue of the times. It is a book of deep convictions, of passion, and of observation; its realistic portraiture, sharp descriptions of places and events, and indomitable spirit of religious quest and moral integrity make it one of the most revealing works of this old Russian literature.

While Avvacum was writing a live idiomatic Russian, various treatises, theological polemics, and eloquent sermons continued to be composed in Church Slavonic. Next to Moscow, Kiev became again an important centre of learning, and its Academy promoted a whole school of ecclesiastic writing. At the same time the Western influence which came mostly through Poland and was particularly felt in the Ukraine, contributed to the spreading of the syllabic form of versification and introduced various new genres of secular prose. Representative of the period was Simeon Polotzky (1629-80), a learned monk who, besides religious works, wrote odes and promoted drama and comedy. Syllabic poetry in a renovated Church Slavonic and the mixed genre of dramatic pieces won the recognition of the educated classes and became the vehicle for the 'high literature.'

The people, however, enjoyed less sophisticated forms of entertainment. Epic ballads continued to be sung in villages, and whoever could read in town and country favoured tales of chivalry, satirical or historical stories, and various fantastic or religio-moralistic narratives written in a plain, often coarse, vernacular. Russian versions of Western and Oriental 'itinerant subjects,' and straight translations, included popular tales about unfaithful wives, and credulous husbands, derived from Renaissance *fabliaux*. From European and Asiatic sources came also jest books, collections of puns and riddles, adaptations of chivalrous songs, and tales of valorous knights and virtuous maidens. The tradition of folklore also flourished in songs. Current events gave rise to new chants. Military settlers, mostly Cossacks, composed ballads and narratives about the conquest of Siberia or the capture of the city of Azov in the South. Some of the popular tales, such as *Eruslan,* a heroic story of Iranian origin, or *The Prince Bova,* of Italian origin, or *Juliana,* the ideal wife and mother, continued to circulate in large printings throughout the eighteenth and nineteenth centuries.

These developments in the folk literature had no connexion, however, with 'polite letters,' and the educated classes continued to ignore the so-called vulgar tales and songs.

But all these phenomena, the romances of chivalry and popular stories and songs, as well as the syllabic poetry and the broadening of genres in the Church Slavonic tradition, were showing the first signs of an imminent change. Most of them were drawing on foreign sources, and this indicated that Russian literature was beginning to move closer to the West.

2. PETER THE GREAT AND THE WESTERN INFLUENCE

THE Westernization of Russia happened most dramatically under Peter the Great (1672-1725). This impetuous Czar founded the Russian empire; built St. Petersburg, its new capital, on the border of the Neva River, close to the Baltic Sea; forcefully threw Russia into the main stream of European civilization; and, thanks to his military victories over the Turks and the Swedes, won his country a place among the leading 'Western nations.' He proceeded with the secularization of the State and Society at a frantic pace and with utter ruthlessness. His was a very definite objective: to break away from the Byzantine tradition of rigidity and isolation, and to promote secular progress in all areas of State organization and secular culture. This he accomplished through authoritarian and often barbarous methods. He crushed in blood the opposition of aristocratic and military groups; and he dispensed torture and death to anyone who stood in his way, including his own son Alexis. To carry out his vast designs, he acted as a tyrant and resorted to force and violence—and herein lies the ambivalent character of his reign—on the one side, reforms, and on the other, the greater burden of suffering on the people.

In this process of Westernization Peter began by borrowing techniques from the more advanced European countries but ended up with acquiring also a whole new crop of cultural values. The importation of watches, wigs, and cannons was soon followed by the German ballet, French poetry, and Italian paintings.

The main impact of Peter's reforms was that science and the arts were abruptly freed from Church domination. Schools were secularized, the alphabet was simplified, and only religious texts continued to be printed in the old Church Slavonic—all other books were, from 1708 on, issued in the new type-face. Peter greatly favoured personal exchange with the West and sent noblemen to study in Europe, where he himself had travelled extensively. He brought to Russia Dutch sea captains, French military engineers, and German artillerists. He also promoted translations of works by European philosophers, scientists, and statesmen, but barred theologians. His approach to literature was strictly utilitarian: he favoured books which he considered useful and wanted writers as assistants in his endeavours. He himself founded the first Russian newspaper, of which he was the printer, the editor, and the chief contributor.

Through this superhuman effort, he did succeed in Europeanizing the upper classes. He forced the old boyars to shave off their long beards and to wear German jackets; young aristocrats were compelled to study foreign languages and adopt French 'politesse.' But while this process of Westernization spread steadily among the land-owners and the new bureaucrats, the large masses of the population were hardly touched by it, and the gap betwen them and their masters grew wider and wider. As a result, educated society became more and more isolated from the peasants and the rest of the nation. And while the masses, crushed by serfdom, poverty, and economic exploitation, lived in conditions of ignorance and general backwardness, clinging solely to the traditions of religion and native folklore, the upper classes spoke and wrote, dressed and ate, thought and worshipped in a manner so foreign to the people as to increase their alienation. Thus the cultural lives of educated society and of the people became as two different currents. They met occasionally but did not actually merge until the Revolution of 1917. The basic problem in Russian life and history, from the reign of Peter the Great up to our day, was this lack of relationship between the so-called vertical culture of the educated society, which in the two hundred and fifty years after the Grand Reformer became magnificently refined—and the popular culture, which was representing the horizontal, widely distributed, and often low in quality.

The full impact of Peter's reforms became apparent in literature only under his heirs. After his death in 1725, and until the end of the century, Russia was governed by a succession of five empresses and three emperors in a turbulent atmosphere of *coups d'état* and military conspiracies; but despite political changes European ways continued to spread extensively and to bring about their cultural transformation.

The man who symbolized the new era, Mikhail Lomonossov (1711-65), was of peasant origin, and his rise demonstrated that Russians were now able to match the highest standards set by European thought. A scholar, he displayed his analytical mind in various treatises; physicist, mathematician, chemist, and geographer, he laid the foundations of Russian secular science and made important discoveries in various fields of research. Not less prominent was his role in literature. He wrote a *Grammar* and *Rhetoric* and formulated a theory distinguishing three principal literary styles: for heroic poetry and serious subjects which require 'force, abundance, magnificence, impressiveness,' he recommended the use of the Church Slavonic. In the middle style (for satires, plays, and 'average' prose writings), he recommended a limited use of Church Slavonic but warned against 'trivial words.' The latter were admitted only in the 'low style,' which covered the spoken language of the common people and was to be reserved for comedies, folk songs, and descriptions of daily occurrences. His classification codified the existing differences and established rules for the school of Russian pseudo-classicism.

Lomonossov himself wrote odes in tonic or accented verse. Together with Vassily Trediakovsky (1703-69), a clumsy, unhappy, but influential poet, he fought against the syllabic versification introduced into Russia from Latin, French, and Polish models (a system based on fixed accents and a definite number of syllables in each line). Russian folklore always resorted to the rhythms of tonic, or eventually, at least, mixed prosody; and Lomonossov understood that the tonic verse, based on the alternation of accents and allowing freedom in the number and order of unaccented syllables (as it does in German and English), was more in the spirit of the Russian language.

This important change in prosody opened a new era for Russian poetry—and Lomonossov's odes greatly contributed to its development. They glorified the Empress Elizabeth, Peter's daughter, and her military victories, or were devoted to meditations about the grandeur of God the Creator. Even though their heavy hyperbolic images and Biblical intonations sounded too solemn and abstract, they had power and sincerity. Today, Lomonossov's poems are too cold and conventional to move us, but in their own time they ranked with the best models of French and German pseudo-classicism, which supplied the artistic standards for various genres in Russian literature. In Russia the national variant of classicism began later, lasting roughly until 1780 and containing more realistic elements than in other countries. This was manifest in the *Satires* of Prince Antiokh Kantemir (1709-44), a poet and diplomat, who aimed at blending life and poetry in his witty portrayals of contemporary Russian mores. Even in the nine tragedies of Alexander Sumarokov (1718-77), one of the founders of the Russian theatre, his strict observance of the unities of place, time, and action and of other conventional rules was mitigated by the numerous realistic traits in his work. His contemporaries called him 'the Northern Racine,' and he certainly imitated the French models of noble passion and sublime conflict; but in his comedies, and particularly in his lyrics and love songs, he drew on Russian folklore and a more earthly presentation of life.

The rapidity with which Russian literature caught up with the West in the first half of the eighteenth century was truly remarkable. Under Empress Catherine (1762-96) the Russian cultural advance increased in speed and volume. The relatively numerous upper class, reared in new educational institutions which also comprised the newly established Moscow University, provided an ever expanding circle of readers and lovers of the fine arts. At the beginning of the century there were only eight periodicals in Russia, but by the end of it there were more than a hundred. Thousands of books were brought out by a steadily growing number of presses; and while the Empire was asserting itself in Europe by a series of military and diplomatic victories, literature was becoming richer and more diversified. Catherine the Second was herself an author. She wrote plays and stories, contributed to satirical journals, and expected her ministers and courtiers to take an interest in poetry. Most of the writers of the eighteenth century in Russia occupied high positions in State administration. The Empress considered their artistic achievements as a service to the nation, and she awarded decorations and financial support to prominent authors. A book of portraits of eighteenth-century Russian writers shows men in brilliant uniforms with ribbons and medals—most of them were generals, admirals, governors, and senators.

The government itself launched magazines, imported books by French authors, organized theatrical performances, and founded publishing houses. Catherine and some of her favourites corresponded with Voltaire, Diderot, and the French encyclopaedists.

Since literature helped to educate the country and to spread ideas and attitudes among the nobility, the government acknowledged its importance. In fact it had the same didactic, utilitarian, and moralistic attitude toward literature as the Church used to have prior to Peter the Great. But by now, ecclesiastical control was replaced by czarist censorship.

The State backed the secularization of literature. This meant that the new style and the new language became the medium of educated society and were officially recognized by the Sovereign and the court.

The literary schools and patterns of the West, as well as all current literary forms from ode and tragedy down to fable and travelogue, were successfully practised in Russia, but they were also 'russified.' In the process of adaption and imitation, the Russians preserved their national characteristics and did not lose their own particular flavour. The evidence for this is in three writers, who, on different levels and surrounded by figures of lesser importance, represent the highest achievements of the eighteenth century in Russia. It should be mentioned that the works of all these writers are closely connected with their general background and with the blossoming of painting, particularly of the art of the portrait; of architecture, which adorned the capital with magnificent

buildings; and of the other fine arts, and of science and
learning.

Gavriil Derzhavin (1743-1816) rose quickly in the bu-
reaucratic hierarchy and was successively appointed gov-
ernor-general of a province, senator, assistant secretary
of the Treasury, and (under Alexander I) minister of
Justice. But he was patronized by Catherine and flattered
by the court not so much because of his administrative
skill (even though he was a good executive), but because
he was the poet-laureate. In fact he became the first great
poet of post-Petrine times. His poems have a sonority, a
fullness of tone, a richness of metaphor, and an oratorical
sway that evoked the spacious rooms of the Imperial
Palace where they used to be recited. The odes in which
he glorified Catherine, and the magnificence of her reign,
reflect verbally a splendid epoch. Although a contemporary reader might find them verbose and uneven, they do
convey an impression of poetic force and intensity.
Moreover, Derzhavin replaced the mathematical loftiness
and abstractness of Lomonossov with oratorical dynamism and sensory concreteness. He also had wit and boasted
of 'telling the truth to the Czars with a smile.' In some
of his poems he sketched bold portraits of his contemporaries; and he succeeded in irritating the authorities with
his impassioned love of justice and hatred of abuses. All
his poetry is permeated by the spirit of independence and
moral courage. This conservative-minded high official became, paradoxically enough, the pioneer of that very civic
poetry which in the nineteenth and twentieth centuries
acquired in Russia strong revolutionary overtones.

Theoretically, Derzhavin followed the precepts of classicism; in practice, particularly while describing idyllic
leisure, good food, the pleasures of the flesh, and the delights of the countryside, he gave free rein to lyrical sub-
jectivism. He showed a whimsical nature and an exuberance of emotion, and he expressed his strong vitality in a
direct, flexible language. In this he breaks a trail for
Karamzin, Batyushkov, and Zhukovsky, the predecessors
and teachers of Pushkin.

While Derzhavin represented the kind of epic and lyric
poetry which was considered by his contemporaries as
the summit of artistic creativity, another literary trend
was highly popular under Catherine II. 'To reform manners through laughter' was the slogan of the second half

of the eighteenth century, and satirical magazines, pamphlets, and comedies waged war against prejudice and ignorance. Greatly influenced by Voltaire, Diderot, Montesquieu's *Persian Letters*, and Swift, Russian fables, tales, comic operas, jingles, and essays began to contain direct or covert criticism of society. This satirical tendency was a sign of the awakening of liberal forces; and it became, in the next century with Gogol, Chekhov, and others, one of the most important trends in Russian letters.

Denis Fonvizin (1745-92), who came from an obscure but cultured family of Muscovite nobles, acted simultaneously as the exponent of the satirical and as a reformer of the Russian theatre. The Empress and her son Paul, the heir apparent, listened to his first comedy, *The Brigadier,* inspired by the Danish playwright, Ludvig Holberg. Fonvizin laughed at the clumsy and backward inhabitants of the provinces, as well as at the pretentious simpletons who dreamt of the world of Paris fashion. His gift for realistic observation and witty epigram found its full expression in *The Young Hopeful,* his masterpiece, and the first truly national Russian play. Fonvizin struck out in it at the superficial imitation of European ways but also hit at the coarseness of the despotic gentry whose welfare was based on serfdom. He sympathized with the underdog, whom he personifies in his comedy as an old nurse who 'gets five roubles a year and gets her face slapped five times a day.' The hero of the play, a half-witted, ill-bred youth, does not want to study because a nobleman has no need of learning. His mother supports him. Why worry about geography, she says, when there are so many postmen and coachmen around?

Despite some farcical notes and a grotesqueness in character portrayal (typical of Russian humour), *The Young Hopeful* was basically a realistic picture of the times. First performed in 1782, it continued for almost two hundred years to be a favourite in the Russian repertory. Its well-defined protagonists and their incisive statements, made in an easy, colloquial style, acquired unfading national popularity. As a social comedy it initiated a tradition followed by Griboyedov, Gogol, Ostrovsky, and Chekhov.

Fonvizin's literary and public activities caused him many tribulations. The Empress ended by finding this

'friend of freedom,' as Pushkin later called him, too independent, almost subversive. His publications were for-
bidden, suspicion hung over his head, and the embittered,
despondent writer turned for consolation to travel and religion. He died after long ill-health at the age of forty-
seven, leaving behind him interesting diaries and travel
notes.

Catherine's change of attitude toward Fonvizin was not
a personal whim but a sign of the times. The French
revolution frightened the Empress and her aristocratic
following, and the authorities devised protective measures against those 'pernicious ideas of the West' which
threatened the autocracy and the nobility. A cleavage developed between the rulers and educated society, one of
the most fateful happenings in Russian history. The government, which in the early '80s financed the translations
of Rousseau and Diderot, looked now with suspicion on
their readers and all the friends of French 'enlightenment.' Freemasons were persecuted and their lodges ordered to be closed. Freedom of the press was banned,
liberal educators were arrested, Derzhavin was censored,
and Fonvizin was not allowed to print his articles. When
Alexander Radishchev (1744-1802), in his *Voyage
from St. Petersburg to Moscow,* published in 1790, attacked serfdom and exposed the inhuman treatment of
peasants and the corruption of police and minor officials,
he was arrested and condemned to death; but the sentence was commuted to exile in Siberia.

Radishchev's work, written with all the fervour of a
sentimental humanitarian who aspired to the emancipation of the serfs and the reform of the whole political
system in Russia, announced the beginning of Russian
radicalism. His exile assumed profound significance: it
symbolized a crucial change in the relations between the
government and educated society. Peter had acted as a
progressive force in creating a class of Europeanized
noblemen and bureaucrats and in promoting its development to the benefit of the State. At that point governmental circles advanced even more rapidly than the society they tried to enlighten. When, finally, an intelligentsia was born and ideas of action, human dignity, social service, culture, and freedom were absorbed and
integrated, there came a period, particularly under Catherine, when the aims of the government and of the

educated minority coincided in scope and pace and a collaboration between the throne and the best elements of the nobility became desirable and possible. But the rift which occurred as a result of the French revolution reversed the situation; and while the rulers tried to put the clock back, supporting rigid autocracy, the awakened society went on and soon found itself in conflict with that same czarist despotism which had started the whole progressive movement. What happened to Radishchev, this talented representative of liberal youth, seemed to stand as a grim warning to the whole class of intellectuals brought to life by Peter's reforms.

3. EARLY NINETEENTH CENTURY

AT the beginning of the nineteenth century the lofty conventions of classical ode and tragedy receded and were finally replaced by melancholy tales, lyrics of heartbreak, and lachrymose digressions on unrequited love. Pre-Romantic sentimentalism increased in both prose and poetry. The great initiator of the new school was Nicholas Karamzin (1766-1826). In his elegantly written novellettes, gentle maidens sighed by murmuring brooks, and idyllic lovers recited sorrowful stanzas in the shade of cemetery trees. His *Poor Liza,* a tale of love and suicide, and his other stories, delighted thousands of readers. No less successful were his *Letters of a Russian Traveller,* in which he drew a picture of revolutionary France and of anti-revolutionary Europe at the turn of the century, 'as seen through a good and tender heart,' as he puts it. Even in the several volumes of his major scholarly work, *History of the Russian State,* which reflected the growth of national consciousness, he displayed a highly subjective approach to people and events. His style, refined, fluent, slightly snobbish, interspersed with neologisms and occasionally with gallicisms, satisfied the expectations of the educated class. They hailed it as their exclusive idiom and also as the medium for a new literary expression. Traditionalists and conservatives, however, were seriously upset by Karamzin's innovations, criticized his mannerisms and his inflated sentences, and accused him, quite unjustly, of subversive tendencies. Their leader Shishkov,

President of the Academy, and Minister of Education under Alexander I, found Karamzin's writing disorderly and in its place defended the theory of the division of styles: he advocated the continued use of Church Slavonic for 'lofty works of imagination,' leaving colloquial language, or 'pure Russian,' for trivial things. He believed that the cause of nationalism and conservatism, which he represented in politics, could be best served by banning all novelty in literature.

Despite all such opposition, Karamzin's school soon gained general recognition. His sentimentalism gradually acquired Romantic overtones, and these became particularly strong in the works of his followers—Zhukovsky and Batyushkov. Both later won their own independent places in Russian poetry.

Vassily Zhukovsky (1783-1852), an indefatigable translator, made remarkable Russian versions of Ossian, Southey, Scott, Byron, Goethe, Schiller, and minor German Romantics. Later critics deprecated the vague dreaminess and mystical mist of his own poetry, but his contemporaries responded to the 'enchanting sweetness' of his verse, and he influenced a whole generation. Some of his poems became anthology pieces and survived across the 'envious gap of centuries,' to use Pushkin's expression.

While Zhukovsky was instrumental in bringing English and German Romanticism to Russians, Konstantin Batyushkov (1787-1855) revived the standards of Hellenic paganism. His delightful, though often highly pessimistic poems, sang the fleeting pleasures of the senses, the loveliness of the visible world, and the poignancy of mortal beauty. The fervour of this passionate man, who could not reconcile his inner contradictions and who ultimately lapsed into madness, counterbalanced the weak and pious resignation of Zhukovsky; but both wrote in the 'new style' and are linked as belonging to the same literary movement, despite all the difference of their temperaments.

Karamzin, Zhukovsky, and Batyushkov, as well as their disciples, were all writing for relatively small audiences. In 1800 a circulation of three to five thousand copies for a work of fiction was considered a great success. The number of those who read and were interested in literature was expanding, although still restricted and small. In these circumstances it seemed that the large popularity of *Fables* by Ivan Krylov (1769-1844) opened a new era; it sold 75,000 copies in the few years before 1812. Krylov wrote as millions spoke and thought, using popular sayings and folklore proverbs and appealing to popular common sense. A large number of his fables were inspired by foreign masters, from Aesop to La Fontaine, but their spirit and wisdom were typically Russian. His tales of mischievous monkeys and greedy wolves, cunning foxes and kind, clumsy bears, merged the animistic pagan spirit of ancient folklore with the down-to-earth realism of the peasant; he also blended the idiom of the masses with the satirical bent of eighteenth-century literature in a masterful way. His humour was direct and unassuming, his jokes salty but never vulgar. Like an old wise farmer, he knew the price of human folly, exposed pretension and stupidity, laughed at ignorance, and shied away from bigotry without ever losing his earthy optimism. He soon became a classic; and the sharp barbs and moralistic sentences of this paternal sage, 'grandfather Krylov,' as his readers called him, became part of Russian speech. Although his popularity lasted over a century, his initial importance was that he wrote for common people living in 'low quarters' when literature was still made for aristocratic drawing rooms.

The battle between archaists and innovators which raged throughout the first quarter of the century was more than a stylistic dispute; it opposed the mentalities and political opinions of two different generations. The reaction which set in during the last years of Catherine's reign and accrued under her son Paul I (assassinated in 1801), seemed to have lost its impact when Alexander I ascended to the throne, but the easing of the regime did not last for long. After a promising beginning, the Czar renounced his humanitarian dreams. Then came Napoleon's invasion of Russia in 1812, the national war of liberation, and with it an outburst of popular patriotism which defeated the French and insured the success of Russian arms in the campaign across Europe. By 1815, after Waterloo and the Vienna Congress, Russia acquired a position of command in the post-Napoleonic world.

Yet a threatening inner conflict sapped her forces at home. The awakening of national consciousness provoked by the war, the expansion of education, the international consolidation of the Empire, and the growth of national wealth gave a new impetus to the educated classes. As they grew in number their cultural needs increased, and literature, music, and the arts flourished and spread from the capital to the provinces. The aspirations of the progressive nobility were, however, thwarted by the grim reality of despotism, serfdom, and social injustice. While liberal ideas were gaining ground among the more en- lightened groups of the nobility, the government, backed by the ever-increasing bureaucracy and a powerful aris- tocracy, became more obstinate and rigid than ever. A large number of young noblemen who served in the Army and went to Germany, Austria, and France dur- ing the 1812-15 campaign, absorbed the ideas of free- dom and equality spread by the French Revolution, and brought home the mood and spirit of political and literary romanticism. They sharply criticized the backwardness of Russia and talked about the need for reforms. Their dis- agreement with their seniors and the revolt of speech in the country of compulsory silence found its artistic ex- pression in *The Folly of Being Wise* by Alexander Griboyedov (1795-1829). This brilliant comedy in verse portrayed Chatsky, a young nobleman who comes to Moscow after a long journey abroad, to find the girl he loves under the influence of a stale and gossipy so- ciety. Her father, Famusov, is interested only in living up to his rank, in giving parties, and in discussing his friends. His secretary, Molchalin, a yes-man, makes his way by vile opportunism, fawning not only before his superiors but even before their dogs. Famusov's intimate, the colonel Skalozub (in whom contemporaries saw the caricature of general Arakcheyev, the cruel and reaction- ary favourite of the Czar), is the 'old soldier' who believes that books are the source of all evil; he recommends the burning of all of them and hails corporals as better teach- ers of youth than Voltaire. In his comedy Griboyedov shows a whole gallery of mummified elders, greedy dowa- gers, feather-brained dandies, and silly officials. Chatsky is choked by the stupidity and priggishness of all those monsters and, disappointed also in love, flees to resume his wanderings.

Although written by a poet who considered himself a Romantic, *The Folly of Being Wise* was surprisingly realistic. Most of its characters were drawn from life—

they talked about current events and quoted facts from the contemporary Russian scene.

The production of this play was banned; but it was avidly read in manuscript copies. In the meantime, young noblemen who felt themselves like Chatsky were forming secret societies for the purpose of overthrowing the government. They failed, however, to change the course of Russian history. After the death of Alexander I, on the day when the new Czar, Nicholas I, was to be enthroned, the conspirators started a military uprising. It was crushed in blood. Five leaders of the revolutionary movement were hanged, and several hundred were imprisoned and sent to Siberia. The Decembrists (the attempted revolt took place on the 14th of December, 1825) initiated the formidable century-long duel between educated society and the government, and the victims became martyrs to the cause of freedom.

All these events showed Russia's coming of age. Its upper classes went through an accelerated process of Westernization, which, in its turn, led to outbursts of energy and creativity.

The one who gave voice to these changes was Alexander Pushkin. He embodied in his work the whole spiritual and artistic growth of Russian society; he revealed the meaning of its past achievements; and, in tracing the road to follow, he became a national writer of the first magnitude.

4. PUSHKIN

A COMMONPLACE of Russian textbooks, that all the currents of the eighteenth century converge in Pushkin and all the rivers of the nineteenth century flow from him, indicates the tremendous impact of his work. Both as a cultural phenomenon and as a poet he is unique in Russian, and perhaps in world literature. He initiated and promoted the widest range of literary genres: he was the author of lyrical poems and dramas, of novels in verse and historical narratives, of critical essays and short stories, of research works and fairy tales, of political epigrams and love songs—there is hardly any field of writing in which he did not leave models of the highest achievement.

In his long poems, dramatic scenes, and prose works he formulated the themes of Russian literature which became recurrent in subsequent writers. The significance of Peter's reforms, the fate of the St. Petersburg empire, the role of power and revolt in Russian history, the rift between Westernized society and the popular masses attached to national traditions, the clash between the aspirations of the little man and the inquisitions of a great State, the issue of the superfluous man, the complexity of human nature, the destructive action and the aesthetic attraction of passion, the moral superiority of the simple heart over the predatory rebel—these and many other subjects gave unusual width and depth to Pushkin's creations. But although it is easy for anyone to appreciate the range and importance of his cultural contribution, it is more difficult for those who do not know Russian to form an adequate idea of his poetic genius. The perennial and ecstatic admiration of his compatriots often seems puzzling or exaggerated to a Western reader. No translation can render that extraordinary coalescence of sound, rhythm, image, and meaning which is the secret of Pushkin's verse and makes it as faultless as a Bach fugue or a Mozart sonata. The words he uses are, for the most part, the simple, plain words of everyday life, and one wonders by what magic enchantment this handful of pebbles acquires the glittering magnificence of precious stones. Only a great poet congenial to Pushkin could transmute his poetry into another language; but so far versions of Pushkin have been made only by scholars, honest amateurs, or even second-rate versifiers; and however useful their efforts are for academic teaching purposes, they are certainly hopelessly pale poetically, and sometimes even trivial. No conclusive evidence can be drawn from these versions and nothing else is left to the Western reader but to accept Pushkin's poetry as an act of faith.

Alexander Pushkin was born in Moscow in 1799 into a family of landed gentry. On his father's side he belonged to old aristocratic stock which was prominent in Russian history since the twelfth century. His beautiful mother was the granddaughter of the Abyssinian princeling Hannibal, once a favourite of Peter the Great; and this African blood was probably responsible for Alexander's passionate nature, his exuberance, and impulsiveness. Like most of the aristocrats of the time, he was brought up by foreign tutors, mostly French, and he spoke and read French even before Russian—his first verse was also in French. But next to this obvious Western influence, he was also exposed to the folk songs and fairy tales of his Russian nurse, who taught him his native tongue in all its purity. He later immortalized her in his poems as the symbol of his country and its people.

At the age of twelve he entered, together with thirty other boys of the best families, the Lyceum at Tsarskoye Syelo (Czar's Hamlet, renamed Pushkin's Hamlet after the Revolution of 1917), which was established by the Emperor to train young aristocrats for high administrative posts. The spirit of the place was liberal and its education excellent. Pushkin learned a great deal of literature, history, ancient and modern languages, and philosophy. His teachers found him brilliant but quick-tempered, kindhearted but full of passion and pride, talented but frivolous. In 1815, when he recited a poem of his own composition in the presence of Derzhavin, at a public examination, the old man wanted to embrace him. Zhukovsky and Karamzin, both of whom Pushkin knew personally, were also struck by the freshness and rhythm of his early poems (still inspired by the French Parny and Voltaire).

After graduation in 1817 Pushkin was appointed to the Foreign Office, but he went there only to draw his salary. He spent most of his time leading the gay and idle life of a man about town and paid substantial homage to Bacchus and Venus. His was a turbulent existence of love affairs, challenges, duels, gambling, and parties. But his lust for pleasure never made him forget his devotion to literature: he wrote numerous poems, madrigals, and jocular verses and became well known in aristocratic salons. He joined the Romantics in their struggle against the archaists, became connected with the 'Arzamas' society, and shared the anti-classical and liberal opinions of his most progressive contemporaries. Many of his young friends belonged to masonic lodges and secret societies, and Pushkin, in serious and satiric poems which made the tour of the capital in manuscript copies, hailed freedom, attacked serfdom, and ridiculed the autocratic regime. This was the cause of his downfall. By order of the authorities he was exiled to the south of Russia. After a trip through the Caucasus and the Crimea he was assigned as a civil servant to Bessarabia and then to Odessa. During the four years of this exile Pushkin continued his antics, but he also found an opportunity for serious literary work. He read avidly and wrote several tales in verse, including the *Caucasian Captive, The Fountain of Bakhchisarai, The Gypsies,* and the first chapter of *Eugene Oneghin;* he also composed beautiful lyrical pieces, and his art reached a new level of maturity. Still, however, he found time for love affairs, fought duels, snubbed his superiors, and expressed openly radical opinions, until finally he was ordered by the authorities to return to his family estate, Mikhaylovskoye, in the northern province of Pskov, under a sort of house arrest. He lived there in forced isolation shared only by his faithful old nurse and a couple of neighbours; and in two years he produced his remarkable *Boris Godunov,* new chapters of *Oneghin,* various tales in verse, and his most beautiful lyrical pieces. The fact of being in a forlorn village during the uprising of the 14th of December, 1825 actually saved him from jail; he would have joined his friends the Decembrists if he had been in St. Petersburg at that time. He was candid enough to tell this to the Emperor, Nicholas I, during an audience some of his influential friends had succeeded in obtaining for him. The Czar, however, liked his frankness and allowed him to reside in Moscow and St. Petersburg.

In 1826, after six years of exile, Pushkin resumed his place in society. This also meant a direct participation in literary life and personal contact with the writers of the time. Despite censorship and strict police surveillance, Pushkin soon became as popular in aristocratic salons as in literary circles. By 1830 author of several volumes of poetry, and already famous, he became active as editor of various periodicals and helped to shape the taste of his contemporaries. His social life was no less successful, but he tired of his feminine conquests and decided to settle down. In 1830 he married Nathalie Goncharova, a strikingly beautiful debutante, and the first years of family life increased his productivity. His tales in prose, including the *Captain's Daughter,* his *History of Pugachev's Rebellion,* his *Bronze Horseman,* and his other poems, as well as minor pieces, emphasized more than ever the leading part he played in Russian letters. But financial worries, the hostility of envious and stupid courtiers, and his ambiguous relationship with the Czar, who, like many other members of the aristocracy, was paying a great deal of attention to Nathalie, then in the bloom of her beauty, entangled Pushkin in a net of intrigue, gossip, and slander. His subordinate situation at the court pained him immensely, and his emotions overrode his caution. When his high-placed foes (including the Dutch ambassador at the Russian Court) resorted to anonymous letters in which Pushkin was called a cuckold, Pushkin challenged one of his wife's suitors, Baron d'Anthes, and was mortally wounded in the ensuing encounter. He died two days later at the age of thirty-seven.

Some critics believe that Pushkin reached the zenith of creativity in his lyrical poetry, in those meditations on nature and death, those confessions of love and remembrances of the past which form the subject matter of his sonnets, and in his other minor forms. Couched mostly in iambic verse, perfectly balanced in rhythm and imagery, they are intense but simple, passionate and moving, yet lucid and concise. Pushkin often depicted adverse circumstances in his own life. He held no illusion about man's condition. Happiness, he said, is impossible, and tranquillity and freedom are the best mortals can hope for. But however sad the accents of his Muse, there is no despair in his poetry. It remains always virile, permeated by a triumphant sense of being. Pushkin is not clouded by approaching death: his wish is instead to be alive, to think and suffer and love, to experience everything under the sun. He is propelled by an inexhaustible curiosity and zest for life. Because his poems reveal such a rare feeling of harmony and verbal balance, some critics have called them 'sunny,' illuminated by the even light of midday. Actually, Pushkin had also explored the nocturnal side of things and was well conscious of the 'devil's part' in his universe. He remarked that 'all things that threaten ruin conceal inexplicable rapture for the heart of man.' But his potent vitality, the brightness of his flame of life, made him akin to the great heroic figures of Greece. His lucidity and sharp, logical intelligence also bring him close to the Greek classics. Pushkin the poet always extolled the human mind and acclaimed 'the sun of reason that makes night's shadows flee.' As a writer and as an individual he moved in the humanistic tradition of Greece, the Renaissance, and the Enlightenment.

Like his beloved Peter the Great, Pushkin was fundamentally secular, and his poetry hardly ever contains religious accents. Its spirit is steadily anti-dogmatic and anti-clerical. Pushkin is much more a pagan than a Christian, more of an 'esprit fort' than a believer, and his work is definitely outside the religious or ecclesiastic tradition of Russian letters. Philosophically he is a positivist and a sensualist. In literature as well as in life he was the relentless enemy of stuffiness, hypocrisy, and artificiality.

His first important long poem, *Ruslan and Liudmila* (1820), was a mock-heroic epic, and the conservatives were horrified at the 'impudence' of the young poet who laughed at the sanctified forms of classicism and showed so much nonchalance, irony, and sensuality while playing with traditional images and devices. The very style of the poem was a novelty, a blending of folklore with the refinements of highly polished verse, a mélange of conversational idiom with lyrical flights. It came at a moment when the war between the Romantics and the Classicists was really fierce and when each periodical was forced to take sides. Those defending the new current hailed Pushkin's work as a victory over the forces of the past. *Ruslan and Liudmila* marked a true change in literary fashion, and Zhukovsky sent Pushkin his portrait with the inscription: 'to the victorious disciple from the vanquished master.' Pushkin's *Fountain of Bakhchisarai* came out with a preface by Prince Viazemsky, one of the foremost defenders of Romanticism, which sounded like the manifesto of the new group. It made Pushkin one of the leaders of the young movement. His other profane and libertine pieces also fought against literary canons and conventional morality, and their aim was to bring poetry down to earth, to make it supple and alive, and to broaden its aesthetic range by rejection of any rules which cramp a poet's freedom. This was probably the initial purpose of his *Eugene Oneghin*, the completion of which took him eight years (1823-31). A long narrative partly inspired by Byron's *Beppo, Don Juan,* and *Childe Harold,* as the anti-religious *Gavriliada* was inspired by Voltaire, it is written in an extremely free, almost loose manner. Descriptive passages alternate in it with lyrical impressions, and meditations of a general nature with realistic pictures.

The hero of the poem, Eugene Oneghin, a sophisticated young nobleman, has been educated in the European fashion and does not know what to do with himself; so, to escape boredom, he poses as a dandy or as a cynic and leads a gay life in St. Petersburg. Nothing, however, can dispel his sense of futility. In a forlorn countryside, he meets a handsome and straightforward girl, Tatiana, who falls desperately in love with the elegant young lion. She is not attractive enough for Oneghin, however, and he rejects her love. He flirts with her sister, who is engaged to his friend, the idealistic poet Lensky, and when Lensky loses his head from jealousy, he kills him in a duel. More than ever disgusted with himself, he travels extensively without ever finding any happiness. A few years later he meets Tatiana, now the wife of a general of high rank and a woman of the world, and, falling in love with her, he is in his turn rejected. Nothing is left for him but to resume his lonely wanderings.

Everything concurred in making *Eugene Oneghin* the first Russian novel, a work of national significance and a masterpiece of poetry. As a narrative it presented colourful tableaux of life in the capital and in the provinces, interspersed with descriptions of native landscapes (which generations of schoolboys have learned by heart), and vivid portraits of Russian men and women, from Tatiana's candid parents to her sister's lover, a pupil of the German Romantics. Oneghin, the main hero, personifies the Europeanized nobleman, abreast with the latest fashions from Paris and London but out of touch with his native soil. This artificial and self-centred young man is the first in the gallery of 'useless men,' one of the main hero-figures of prerevolutionary Russian fiction. Tatiana possesses the organic unity he lacks; she is in perfect harmony with her Russian environment. Their conflict hinges on the problem of genuine feelings and moral courage; and Oneghin's failure to win Tatiana during his second encounter with her assumes a symbolic significance: a healthy concept of truth and duty triumphs over cynicism and Western superficiality. Half a century after the publication of the poem, Dostoevsky, in his speech on Pushkin in 1880, analysed the implications of the work and proclaimed it a national poem: Tatiana became for him one embodiment of Russian simplicity and integrity.

The contemporaries of Pushkin sometimes did not catch the deeper meaning of the poem, but they enjoyed its beauty, grace, and novelty. It was a multi-level composition. With unflagging sensitivity Pushkin discusses in it varied subjects, from ballet to philosophy, from love to literature, indulges in melancholic remembrances, personal confidences, and objective descriptions, makes most amazing digressions, and combines seriousness with gaiety in a truly Romantic fashion. In general, the mixture of the trivial with the sublime and of the lyrical with the ironic, which the Romantics used as a challenge to fixed genres, was fully exploited by Pushkin in his struggle to renew Russian poetry. But paradoxically enough, even though *Eugene Oneghin* as a poem belonged to the new school, its hero, Oneghin, signified Pushkin's rejection and refutation of the Romantic 'dark hero'; and the work actually was Russia's first realistic novel in verse.

Between 1820 and 1823 Pushkin fell under the influence of Byron and even learned English in order to be able to read his beloved poet in the original. But this infatuation did not last long; and after having written *The Caucasian Captive*, obviously inspired by the Byronic mood, he looked for his own path. He disliked the supernatural and the unbelievable and, despite his own fiery temperament, shied away from exaggeration. As we know from his correspondence, he soon saw through Byron's affectation and reproached him for making each of his heroes merely the portrayal of some aspect of his own personality. Moreover, he questioned the 'dark hero' and his rebellion against society. In *The Gypsies,* Aleko, a Romantic hero, leaves the city and seeks happiness among strong primitive men. He is in love with a Gypsy girl and when she is unfaithful to him, kills her as well as her suitor. But instead of praise he gets only blame from the chief of the tribe. The 'noble savage' rejects him: 'leave us, proud man, you are wicked and bold whereas we are kind and peaceful. No need have we of bloodshed and groans.' Here again, as in *Eugene Oneghin,* Romantic passions are opposed by the virtues of simplicity and kindness.

Pushkin joined the Romantic movement and fought in its ranks very much like Stendhal, for whom Romanticism was identified with liberalism and simply meant 'modern literature versus old literature.' He often described passions and dramatic situations, particularly in his short, tense stories, in which he tells us about ambitious and superstitious gamblers (*Queen of Spades*), disillusioned adventurers (*The Shot*), or gentlemen robbers (*Dubrovsky*). But he presents extraordinary incidents and tempestuous emotions in a most classical style. However fiery his subject matter, he, as a narrator, remains poised and in full control of his material. When Byron was replaced by Shakespeare in his affection, he wrote *Boris Godunov*, a sequence of scenes from the times of trouble in the seventeenth century, a most dramatic and involved period of Russian history; and in his own words he aimed at 'truthfulness of representation' and took 'the fate of man and the destiny of a people' as his basis of tragic conflict. This vast chronicle was perfectly proportioned and sober in its outline. The same can be said of all his dramatic scenes, as well as of his excellent historical novelette *Captain's Daughter*, in which he leads his hero through the flames of the Pugachev rebellion, without ever lapsing into the melodramatic and always following the rules of economical and orderly composition. In general, nothing was more remote from Pushkin than a Bohemian carelessness and lack of proportions.

Pushkin shared the Romantic belief in unconscious inspiration as the real essence of art and demanded complete freedom for poetic creation. In several poems he expressed his credo: 'to depend on nobody, to serve and please none but himself'; yet at the same time he compared the poet to an echo, or rather to the prophet whose words burn the heart of mortals; and in the proud poem 'A Monument I Reared' (inspired by Horace), he foretold his future fame and claimed his name would be cherished by all of Russia, because 'I awakened kind feelings with my lyre, because in my ruthless age I glorified freedom and invoked mercy for the vanquished.' Even though it would be useless to look for a moral lesson or a definite philosophy in Pushkin's works, it is undeniable that his sympathies were always with the humble and that he condemned the predatory. In *Mozart and Salieri* he contended that true genius is essentially moral and therefore incompatible with crime. There is nothing metaphysical in Pushkin's earthly and secular poetry, in which pagan sensuality often drowned Christian motives. Love of clarity and balance—'man is the measure of all things'—runs through all his work. Politically, he went from youthful radicalism to the acceptance of monarchy in his late twenties, but toward the end of his life he resumed his critical attitude toward autocracy, and he always remained a liberal, an enemy of despotism, and a lover of freedom.

Few men of Pushkin's time in Russia absorbed European culture as fully as he did. He studied the classics, had an extensive knowledge of great writers from Dante to Cervantes, from Shakespeare to Milton, and from Goethe to Voltaire, and he was widely read in contemporary European literature. 'I love Europe with all my heart,' he said, and this love was enhanced by knowledge and intuition. He had an amazing capacity for depicting different countries and historical periods and for catching the basic traits of national character—his dramatic settings range from medieval Germany (*The Covetous Knight*) to Renaissance Scotland (*The Feast During the Plague*), from Italy (*Angelo*), or from Spain of the Inquisition (*The Stone Guest*) to eighteenth-century Austria (*Mozart and Salieri*). At the same time this convinced and enlightened Westerner was an unmistakable champion of the Russian spirit. Dostoevsky claimed that Pushkin's very capacity for universality was a typically Russian trait, that to be a true Russian one must strive for universality and understand all the other peoples of Europe. In any case, Pushkin deliberately sought to express a national consciousness. His interest in Russian history, from *Boris Godunov* to the *Captain's Daughter*, showed how preoccupied he was with the problem of the nation's destiny. He declared himself a staunch defender of Peter's reforms and glorified the great Czar to the extent of becoming his bard. In *Poltava* he represented him as a victorious semi-god. In the *Bronze Horseman* (1833), one of the most important Russian poems of the nineteenth century, he identified the image of the Emperor with the equestrian statue of Peter erected on the bank of the Neva—the steed on its hind legs, ready to leap, in the formidable grip of the rider is compared to Russia held in by the Czar. The poem describes the flood of 1824, which threatened to submerge St. Petersburg, the artificial creation of the impetuous ruler, and which actually destroyed the happiness of a small employee, Eugene, who goes out of his mind, challenges Peter, and perishes in a nightmare. He sees the bronze statue pursue him through the inundated streets of the capital. Symbolically, Peter, who defied God and nature, wins and crushes the individual for the glory of the State. Thus Pushkin accepts the St. Petersburg empire and grants it historical justification, even though all his sympathies are with its victims. The tragedy of the little man in the desperate struggle with historical fate, as put by Pushkin, was destined to become one of the main themes of Russian literature.

Pushkin felt Russia as a whole, and was confident of her future. A national poet, a reformer of Russian poetry, a renovator of its literature, he embodied the inner force of a country which accepted and tried to assimilate the Western legacy, and was yet ready to enrich it with its own accomplishments. In Pushkin, Russian literature also acquired the consciousness of its own peculiarities and realized its own originality. Peter the Great bridged Russia and Europe in a material, physical sense; Pushkin did it spiritually and artistically. The first national poet of Russia, he is also its first writer of universal appeal, fame, and importance.

5. LERMONTOV

PUSHKIN'S death struck educated society a terrible blow, but high officials did not view the event with the same eye. When a St. Petersburg newspaper appeared with a black border announcing that 'the Sun of Russian poetry has set,' Count Benckendorf, the Chief of the political police, exclaimed: 'Why all this fuss about an individual who did not even occupy an important post!' Court circles and aristocratic conservatives jeered and joked about 'that rhymester with too beautiful a wife.' Titled snobs and defenders of Baron d'Anthes were, however, severely rebuked in a poem which made the rounds of the capital in manuscript copies. It glorified the deceased poet and called his revilers 'a hungry throng who crowd the Royal Court, base lovers of corruption, stranglers of Freedom, Genius, Glory.' An old dowager sent a copy of this poem to the Emperor with the inscription: 'Here is an appeal to revolution.' Nicholas I was at once incensed, and ordered the arrest of the subversive author. He proved to be Mik-

hail Lermontov, a twenty-three-year-old Hussar officer in
the Imperial Guard. Shortly afterwards he was reduced
in rank and sent to an infantry regiment at the front line
in the Caucasus, where Russians were still waging war
against unpacified native tribes. By the time Lermontov
departed, his name was well known in the literary world.
Thus his exile marked the beginning of a poetic career
which was as brilliant as it was brief.

Mikhail Lermontov, born in 1814, claimed that his ancestors descended from the Scottish lairds of Learmont
and the Spanish dukes of Lerma, and came to Russia only
in the seventeenth century; his father, however, was a
poor and frivolous army captain who married a rich
heiress. She died when her son was three, and he was
brought up on the family estate in Central Russia by
Madame Arsenieva, his maternal grandmother. She adored
Mikhail but could not stand Captain Lermontov, and she
hardly ever let him see his son. Mikhail was a precocious
boy, dreamy and wilful, self-centred and impulsive. He
started writing poetry at the age of eight, and fell violently in love at ten. After an illness his grandmother took
him to a spa in the Caucasian mountains, and the savage
beauty of this region impressed him forever. Tutors and
governesses taught him Latin and Greek, French and
German, and later English. In 1827 he entered a prepar-
atory school in Moscow; devoured works on Napoleon,
whom he worshipped; read Scott, Moore, Shelley, and
Byron; and became an ecstatic lover of Pushkin's poems.
It is a fact that by the age of fifteen he had not only
written a number of poems, tales, and dramas, but had
also made plans and drafts for all the works that later
made him famous. He was only fifteen, too, when he composed some of the anthology pieces, such as 'The Angel,'
that all Russian children learn by heart. What makes it
even more striking is that his style, his mannerisms, and
the main traits in his versification were all completely
formed during his childhood. By the age of seventeen he
had written 300 lyrics, fifteen long poems, three dramas,
and a novelette.

He had, however, an adolescence clouded by all sorts
of complexes. His passions were wild, yet he had an icy
logic and could dissimulate his emotions under the mask
of sarcasm and distant irony. Shy and aggressive, sensual
and idealistic, kind-hearted and often cruel, he suffered

from a sense of inferiority and was subject to fits of despondency. No wonder that between 1827 and 1834 he felt strongly attracted by Byron. It seemed to him that they had in common the spirit of non-conformity, of demonic pride, and of rebelliousness. But Lermontov's Byronism was not a pose. He loved and imitated Byron's works because of the similarity of their moods and passions; but as he said himself in a revelatory poem, 'No, I am not Byron, I am different, and so is my unknown fate; like him I am a persecuted wanderer, but I have a Russian soul.'

There is no doubt that unhappiness in love sharpened the edges of Lermontov's contradictory personality. It is not certain whether it was Nadezhda Ivanova, the daughter of a Moscow playwright, or the aristocratic Varenka Lopukhina (both of whom were married in the early thirties of the century) who inspired all his songs of unrequited love. In any case, this first disillusionment marked him for life. Later he seemed to take his revenge on women, and his numerous love affairs followed the same pattern, that of a game of seduction; once at the finish he was no longer interested in the prize. This urge for domination would be interrupted by a sudden need for tenderness or by fits of apathy and boredom.

After a short period of study in Moscow University, where he came into contact with German idealistic philosophy and Russian radicalism, he went to St. Petersburg and in 1832 joined the Imperial Guard Hussars. He aspired to become a worldly and social success. Vain and brilliant, he soon acquired the reputation of a firebrand and, despite his ugliness, of a Don Juan. At this point he was writing libertine poems of a kind his comrades in arms could enjoy; but by 1835 he had turned to more serious literary endeavours, and a couple of his unsigned poems appeared in periodicals. Only after his arrest and exile in 1837, however, did he start publishing his works regularly, and they gained him immediate success and fame.

In 1839 Lermontov was granted a pardon and resumed his life in St. Petersburg, this time not only as a gay Hussar in search of adventure, but also as a poet, and a victim of political persecution.

In 1840 he quarrelled with the son of the French ambassador to Russia over a beautiful lady and challenged him to a duel. The incident was immediately reported to the Emperor and Lermontov was again arrested and exiled to the Caucasus. Some biographers contend that Nicholas I had personal reasons for disliking the poet, others speak of a duchess whom Lermontov had offended. In any case, those at court were openly hostile to him. In the following months the critics acclaimed his poems and his novel *A Hero of Our Own Times*. Hopes were expressed that Lermontov would become the heir of Pushkin. But in July 1841 a row with his friend Martynov (both were courting the same young girl) led to a duel, and Lermontov was killed. He was twenty-seven years old. His posthumous glory increased rapidly. A few years after his premature death he was hailed unanimously as Russia's second great poet, and his works thereafter became classics.

They were so subjective, so personal that they sounded like autobiography or lyrical confession. He projected himself not only in his shorter poems, which ranged from passionate youthful outbursts to mature pieces of poetic perfection, but also in his dramas such as *The Masquerade* (1835), and in his long narratives in verse (*The Novice, The Demon),* which contained actual transcripts of his own feelings and thoughts. They remained also the fullest expression of Russian Romanticism. Lermontov was a Byronic Romantic, not by imitation or literary affinity, but by temperament. Ambivalence was inherent in his character, and he was split by contradictions. In early adolescence, in 'The Angel,' he spoke of a young soul about to be born and carried through celestial fields by a singing angel; the heavenly sounds sank deep into her and later she languished on earth tormented by strange desires, unable to replace the echo of divine melody with dull human songs. This conflict between dream and reality, between the beautiful vision and the coarseness of life, became Lermontov's main theme. He rejects the world he lives in and seeks an escape from triviality and contingencies. The hero of his remarkable poem *The Novice* (*Mtzyri* in the original) flees, runs away from his monastery and wanders in the wilderness of the Caucasus, face to face with savage nature. He experiences hunger and solitude, he fights wild beasts, he enjoys freedom and danger. At the end of his escapade he dies happy, because his brief moment of intense existence has been worth much more than a long life of dullness.

Arbenin in *The Masquerade* challenges society and affirms his right to establish his own good and evil; the recurrent image of Demon becomes a symbol of Lermontov's rebellion against God and the Universe, and a reflection of his own self. In his most celebrated poem, *The Demon,* which has all the enchantment of an Oriental legend, the 'Exile from Paradise' is a 'melancholy spirit.' Like the soul in 'The Angel,' he remembers the songs of heaven and suffers from his isolation. His only hope for salvation is in his love for Tamara, a beautiful Georgian girl. She is engaged, but the Demon kills her fiancé; she flees to a convent, but he tempts her in dreams; and when finally he seduces her and holds her in his arms, the kiss of the Demon destroys the mortal maiden, and God's angel takes her soul upward, while the Exile is left to his eternal despair. Lermontov left several drafts of this dramatic work (1833-41), in which passions of pride, love, and rebellion are projected against the majestic and exotic scenery of the Caucasian mountains, which he glorified in his work.

Even though his verse was, as he said himself, 'often filled with bitterness and anger' and extolled 'the wonderful ecstasy of defiance,' it mellowed with time and his pessimism and sarcasm were less pronounced in the last years of his life. Blue skies shone through the broken stormy clouds in his lyrics, and he yearned for a reconciliation with God and the world. Moreover, Lermontov, the most Romantic and passionate of Russian poets, displayed a growing interest in realistic narrative. His two historical poems, *Borodino,* an epic evocation of the great battle of Napoleon's invasion of Russia in 1812, and his *Lay of the Czar Ivan the Terrible and the Merchant Kalashnikov,* written in the manner of folklore epic song, as well as some other minor items, were definitely conceived and executed in a new vein. So was his novel in prose, *A Hero of Our Own Times* (1840). His semi-autobiographical hero, Pechorin, a young officer, wilful and intelligent, with a variety of experience behind him, does not know how to channel the 'enormous forces' he senses in himself. Since all purposeful and useful activity except soldiering is denied him in the autocratic police-state of Nicholas I, he wastes his energy in bravado and senseless adventures, ruins women who love him, and finally is thoroughly disgusted with himself and with the world in general. As the title of the novel indicates, Pechorin is the child of his century, and his inability to make use of his rich potentialities can be explained in terms of the social environment.

A whole generation handicapped by serfdom and political reaction, and choked by inactivity, was condemned to this useless existence. But Lermontov went further than Pushkin in his analysis of the superfluous individual. Pechorin has qualities Oneghin lacked completely. He possesses energy and pride, and he can be aggressive and purposeful, even though he aims at futile victories and is mostly propelled by vanity. Lermontov treats him with cool objectivity verging on irony, and the result is a debunking of the 'dark hero.' The poet actually dealt a mortal blow to one of the most popular literary conventions of that very Romantic movement of which he was the main representative exponent. This is the paradox of Russian Romanticism: Pushkin, while declaring himself the champion of the new attitude, rejected and destroyed the Byron myth and refused to accept Romantic traits as human virtues; and Lermontov, in his turn, did not spare Pechorin, but made an *exposé* of his egotism and artificiality. It looked as if the most important Russian Romantics were determined to divest the Romantic hero of all his charm and attraction. Not unlike Heine, Lermontov seemed determined to treat the Romantic hero as a clinical case, to expose him as a social type, and to analyse him as a moral and psychological problem. As a proud man who transgresses the accepted code of behaviour and asserts his right to do as he pleases, Pechorin is actually the forerunner of Dostoevsky's rebels, from Raskolnikov to Ivan Karamazov. All of them are passionate and energetic and have none of the weaknesses of the superfluous man: they all want to be, like Pechorin, beyond good and evil. Lermontov, like Dostoevsky, follows certain themes of Pushkin and confronts the predatory, self-willed Pechorin with his humble friend, the simple-minded major Maxim Maximovitch. A man of warmth and integrity, the major is a 'simple heart' who is mistreated by the ambitious Pechorin, but though condemned to play secondary parts in life, he acquires a moral superiority over his brilliant opponent.

In general, moral problems are central to Lermontov's prose and poetry. Why is man attracted by evil? What are the hidden sources of our actions? Why do some individuals reject the existing order of things and try to surpass human limitations? These and similar questions were always worrying Lermontov, and they constantly recur in all his work. This moral preoccupation as well as the realistic tendencies in his last writing, make Lermontov a very peculiar kind of a Romantic. His example confirms the observation that Russian Romanticism carried strong national characteristics. In comparison with their European counterparts, Russian Romantics laid less stress on the extraordinary, the bizarre, and the grandiose, and turned earlier towards a realistic representation of life. From the beginning they were more interested in social conflict and moral anxiety. Their philosophical non-conformity contained a definite criticism of existing social and political conditions. In that sense Lermontov, 'the nocturnal luminary of Russian literature,' as Merezhkovsky called him, denies Pushkin's affirmations. The literary manner of the two was very different. Lermontov's verse was nervous, muscular, and dynamic. The intermittent rhythms of his poems with their abundant masculine rhymes had strength rather than consonance and harmony. In comparison with Pushkin's luminosity and verbal perfection, Lermontov's poems contain disturbing obscurities and symbolic undercurrents. The prophetic grief of this young poet, his contradictions, his despondency and idealistic aspirations, his genuine force and restlessness preserved the appeal of his poems for many generations; and at the end of the century the symbolists saw in him one of their forerunners.

Pushkin and Lermontov were the two greatest poets at a time when poetry in general was blooming in Russia. Between 1820 and 1850 a whole generation of excellent poets followed the masters and raised the standards of Russian verse to unprecedented heights. During Pushkin's lifetime, poems by Tiutchev, Baratynsky, Yazykov, Koltzov, and many others were published and appreciated by an ever-growing public of poetry lovers. Although the bulk of Tiutchev's work belongs to a later period, the others formed a compact group often called 'Pushkin's Pleiad.' Some of them were his schoolmates, such as the solemn, heavy-footed Romantic Decembrist Wilhelm Kuechelbecker (1797-1846), who died blind in Siberian exile, Anton Delvig (1798-1837), the lover of Greco-Roman classics and the editor of Russia's first *Literary Gazette*. Some of Pushkin's seniors gave him full support in his struggle for new forms against the artistic conservatives, notably Prince Peter Viazemsky (1792-1878), a Romantic poet, a sharp polemist, a witty critic, and a Czarist dignitary. Others who belonged to the rather large group of Pushkin's friends and followers still preserved their individuality as poets. Eugene Baratynsky (1800-44) wrote: 'My Muse is no raving beauty but one is struck by the uncommon expression of her face.' His wide brow was that of an intellectual, and his poems dealt with themes in idealistic philosophy and with abstract concepts. He believed that only imagination and the creative arts can overcome the restrictions of matter and death, was very pessimistic about the 'common man' and society, and dreaded the inevitable advent of an 'iron age' of mechanical standardization. With other members of the group 'Lovers of Wisdom,' such as Prince Vladimir Odoevsky, Dimitri Venevitinov, and partly Karolina Pavlova (the first Russian woman poet), Baratynsky had felt the impact of German Romantic philosophers, particularly of Schelling, who, together with Hegel, had a large following in Russian educated society.

A different trend was represented by Nikolai Yazykov (1803-46), the bacchic poet of youth, of sensual pleasures, of wine and women. His exuberant pagan songs enlivened the gatherings of Russian students for a century; and their value lay in their sonorous vigour and throbbing vital rhythms.

Although most of 'Pushkin's Pleiad' belonged to the nobility, two poets of the period came from the lower classes: Vladimir Benediktov (1807-73), a loud and superficial Romantic, and Alexei Koltzov (1809-42), a peasant whose unaffected poems appeared as naïve and charming as wild flowers. The Romantics, highly interested in folklore, praised Koltzov's songs extravagantly as genuine expressions of the national soul.

The wide range of poetic genres, the remarkable attainments in form and rhythm, the attention paid to poets by the critics as well as the interest shown by readers, resulted in the large circulation of poetic works, and made poetry the main literary force of the period. The influence of these poets was to be felt for many decades to come. Only at the end of 1840 did the situation change and prose come to the fore—and this coincided with the decline of Romanticism as a movement and with the emergence of the realistic or 'natural' school, the elements of which were present already in Pushkin's tales. In this literary evolution common to all countries, Russia's progress, which trailed a little behind that of Europe, was determined at every stage by her special social, political, and cultural conditions.

6. GOGOL AND THE NATURAL SCHOOL

A GREAT many writers tried their hand at prose in the first three decades of the nineteenth century. The sentimental tale initiated by Karamzin was still in fashion, and thousands of readers, mostly women, shed tears over broken hearts or thrilled to some new 'dark hero.' Historical narratives became very popular and Michael Zagoskin (1789-1852), author of the best seller, *Yuri Miloslavsky,* or Ivan Lazhechnikov (1792-1869), author of *The House of Ice,* presented a pageantry of Russia's past after the manner of Sir Walter Scott. The grandiloquent adventures of passionate heroes in exotic settings in the tales of the Decembrist, Alexander Bestuzhev-Marlinsky (1797-1837), found thousands of readers, as did other minor Romantic works. A more realistic spirit, combined with a satirical bent, was obvious in the picaresque novels of A. Weltman (1800-70) and those of Vassily Narezhny (1780-1835), the author of *Russian Gil Blas* or *The Adventures of Prince Chistiakov* and other pictures of provincial life. All these writers, with Kvitka Osnovianenko (1779-1843), prepared the ground for Gogol; and although some of them are considered his predecessors, it was only in Gogol's works that Russian prose affirmed its artistic originality.

Son of a small landowner, Nikolai Gogol was born in 1809 and spent his childhood on the small family estate near Poltava and part of his adolescence in the Nezhin Lyceum for noblemen. The easygoing atmosphere of the Ukrainian south, with its folklore traditions, and the slow

pace of a sleepy provincial town formed the major stock
of memories which Gogol drew on for his work. A dreamy
imaginative youth with a headful of odd ideas, Gogol believed he was called to become an actor. In 1828 he went
to St. Petersburg, failed to get on the stage, had to earn
his living as a petty government clerk and devoted himself to writing. His Romantic poems were a fiasco, and he
turned to prose. In 1831-2 he published two volumes of
Evenings on a Croft near Dikanka, a collection of stories
based on Ukrainian folklore, half fairy tales, half legends,
influenced by the German Romantics L. Tieck and E. T.
Hoffmann. In most of them scurvy devils tried their wiles
on carefree and robust Cossack peasants, perhaps spoil-
ing a love affair but in the end being defeated by some
shrewd blacksmith or cunning maid. While *May Night, St.
John's Eve, Sorochintsy Fair,* and *The Bewitched Spot*
are full of genuine gaiety and poetic sensitiveness, others
such as *Terrible Revenge,* a story of incest and murder,
are really Romantic horror tales. A curious blend of the
supernatural and the comic pervades *Mirgorod,* a sequel
to the first collection. It contains *Viy,* a legend about a
beautiful witch who seduces and ruins Thoma, a semina-
rist. Thoma attends an orgy of devils and ghosts in a dese-
crated church and sees Viy, the king of gnomes, whose
glance kills, and whose iron eyelids droop to the very
ground. Romantic devices like the opposition of humour
to horror, the interplay of contrasts, and the colourful
background of national folklore showed in all those collections, which were a sensational literary success. Yet,
in a new way, some of his stories departed from Romantic patterns and dealt with the 'low trivialities' of provincial life, depicting average undistinguished men and
containing a wealth of exact detail. Gogol introduced to
his puzzled and delighted readers funny and slightly pathetic characters: a shy self-effacing youth dominated by
an energetic elderly relative (*Shponka and His Aunt*);
two empty-headed neighbours of the small landed gentry,
who break their long friendship over a trifle, become ac-
cursed enemies, and spend the rest of their lives in courts
and litigation (*How Ivan Ivanovich Quarrelled with Ivan
Nikifirovich*); an idle and innocuous couple whose un-
eventful existence, from birth to death, was spent in vege-
tative placidity (*Old-fashioned Landowners*). In all these
stories Gogol displayed an extraordinary gift for observa-

tion, reproducing sounds, smells, and shapes with an almost uncanny verbal and phonetic brilliancy. Like a torrent in bright sunshine, his prose scintillated in its rapid flow, shimmering, alive, and irrepressible. But this master, who appeared intoxicated by his own words and played with them like a juggler, seemed terrified by the boredom and meanness which he depicted. He began to feel some mystical horror before the stupidity and coarseness of most men's lives.

He tried to find escape in heroic sagas of the past and in the idealization of Men of Might. *Tarass Bulba,* a short historical novel, recalls the seventeenth-century Ukrainian Cossacks, their military community of free men on an island of the Dnieper, and their wars against the Poles and the Turks. Tarass, the old leader, kills his younger son, who has betrayed the Cossacks by falling in love with a beautiful Polish girl and joining the enemy. When his older son Ostap is captured by the Poles and put to death, Tarass, hidden in the crowd, watches the execution and promises eternal revenge. The whole pageant of Cossack chivalry is very much in Sir Walter Scott's tradition. The exaggerated Romanticism of the whole book is relieved by some delightfully comic passages, by deft sketches of secondary characters, and by beautiful descriptions of nature, particularly of the Southern steppe.

After some unsuccessful attempts at historical research and teaching, Gogol returned to writing novelettes. By 1838 he had published several St. Petersburg tales. In all of them commonplaces of daily life were intermingled with the uncanny or the supernatural, frequently as in the works of E. T. Hoffmann, whom Gogol greatly admired. The painter Piskarev, the hero of *Nevsky Prospect,* believes a girl he met in the street to be the embodiment of purity and beauty, but she leads him straight to a brothel; while his friend Pirogov, immune to dreams and torments, seeks the earthly favours of a buxom baker's wife. The smug Major Kovalev (*The Nose*) discovers one morning that his nose had suddenly disappeared and runs to the police to recover it by legal means. In *The Portrait* (first draft), the young painter Chertkov is corrupted by money and success, which the devil has offered him; and in *The Memoirs of a Madman,* a down-trodden petty clerk imagines himself king of Spain.

Instead of the inconsequential laughter of his youth,

Gogol now used his humour as a satirical weapon, exposing reality through the grotesque and making dreams and fantastic visions emerge out of comic situations. His tales at this point reflected the anxiety of a weird and frustrated mind. Triviality now appeared to him the very expression of evil. Petty ugly demons populate his universe of confusion and imbecility. In another story, *The Overcoat,* which was published in 1842 but which belongs to the group of St. Petersburg tales, his sense of emptiness is mitigated by pity. Its hero, Akaki Akakievich, a humble office copyist, has but one dream: a new overcoat, a palpable evidence of human dignity. He gets it at the price of sacrifice and privation, but the very night he wears it for the first time, he is held up and robbed of his most precious possession. In vain he solicits the help of the police and the intervention of a Very Important Person—the latter simply throws him out, and the unhappy Akaki Akakievich dies from grief. But his ghost haunts the frosty streets of the capital, and one night pulls the overcoat off the shoulders of that Very Important Person who mistreated him. Thus poetic justice is done, and the ghost disappears for ever.

The impact of this semi-fantastic story was enormous, although contemporaries did not pay much attention to its supernatural ending, written as it was in a mocking, jocular manner. Gogol's pity for the underdog, his representation of the insignificant 'little man,' his feeling for social, or maybe universal injustice, inherent in the fate of the 'humiliated and wronged,' and his Christian compassion for the weak and meek—these basic themes of Russian literature were all present in this sentimental grotesque. Dostoevsky contended that the whole tradition of Russian prose could be traced back to *The Overcoat.* He himself, as well as dozens of others, certainly were greatly influenced by Gogol.

Gogol hardly realized the impact of his own work. He usually wrote in a trance, in a fit of inspiration, obeying an unconscious impulse, like a sleepwalker; and many of his pages sound like the transcription of a dream. Only when his first draft was ready did Gogol work on it, rewriting separate scenes (sometimes from five to eight times), carefully choosing the right words, and polishing up the characterizations. Here again, he was yielding to his ambivalence. He was an ambitious writer, vain and very proud of his unique position in Russian letters; and he loved fame and thought highly of his vocation. But he always went further than he wanted to with his pen, and he was sincerely mystified by the repercussions of his works. There was a gap between his initial intention and the actual artistic result. This was, for instance, the case with his comedy *The Inspector General*. Its plot (as well as the plot of *Dead Souls*) was suggested by Pushkin, and Gogol, who was very interested in the theatre (he left several plays, among them the delightful and obliquely autobiographical *The Marriage*), set to work with enthusiasm. In 1836 *The Inspector General* was produced in St. Petersburg before a stunned audience. It provoked such a stir and controversy that all educated society became divided into revilers and defenders of the new comedy. This was a complete surprise to the poor author, who, after some clumsy attempts at self-justification, became so distressed that he fell ill and fled abroad.

The action of the comedy takes place in a small provincial town ruled by a coarse, money-grabbing mayor and a gang of dishonest and ignorant officials. They all mistake Khlestakov, a young impecunious scoundrel, for the anticipated Inspector General from St. Petersburg. Khlestakov exploits the confusion, takes bribes, puts the fear of God into frightened officials, becomes engaged to the mayor's daughter, and then departs, not without sending a letter to his friend in which he laughs at his dupes. The letter is intercepted at the post office and later read aloud at the mayor's house in the presence of dazed victims, who at the end are told that the true Inspector General has just arrived.

Gogol used this simple story of 'qui pro quo' or mistaken identity as a vehicle for portraying memorable characters: the harsh and crude Mayor; his flirtatious wife; his empty-headed daughter; the two silly landowners, Russian Humpty Dumpties; the prying Postmaster; the melancholic head of the hospital where patients, according to his slip of the tongue, are cured like flies; and finally Khlestakov, the liar, the shallow impostor, the vulgar symbol of universal emptiness. Despite Gogol's love for caricature, audiences and readers recognized his characters as familiar figures, as part of Russian reality. They seemed so true and so typical that *The Inspector General* was immediately extolled as a social satire and as a na-

tional comedy. Its political significance as a condemnation of the existing regime seemed to outweigh all its other
merits. Since its plot and characters were taken from
everyday life and its language was the colloquial, at times
coarse, idiom of the half-educated people, the great critic
Belinsky called Gogol the head of the 'natural school,'
and this tag remained attached to him for almost a century. Taking their cue from Belinsky, all the critics in
Russia and abroad hailed Gogol as a realist, without add-
ing that his realism was of a very peculiar and personal
brand.

While the controversy over *The Inspector General* was
raging in Russia, Gogol was travelling in Europe, finally
settling in Rome. He wrote various explanations of his
comedy, claimed that laughter was his positive hero,
made confusing remarks about *The Inspector General*
being the symbol of the Last Judgement, and went to
great lengths to prove that his satire contained nothing
subversive. In fact, he was a loyal subject of the Emperor,
a faithful son of the Church, and had nothing whatever
to do with revolutionary tendencies. But the inner crisis
he suffered from was deeper than the simple anxiety of a
conservative who discovers that his works are helping
the radicals. Gogol wanted to uphold the didactic traditions of Russian literature. He dreamed of teaching, of
being of use to his contemporaries, of performing a social
service. Yet he had strong doubts whether the kind of
work he was capable of producing would well serve his
purpose.

In his Roman retirement he continued writing *Dead
Souls*. He wanted it to be a gay picaresque novel, but
when, before leaving Russia, he read the first chapter to
Pushkin, the poet laughed at first, then remarked: 'Lord,
how sad is our Russia.' And now, after Pushkin's death,
Gogol was more than ever aware that his was 'a laughter
through tears,' and he was beset by all sorts of moral and
religious anguish. He was of frail physique, he never had
any sexual relations with women, and he was tormented
by pathological complexes, real and imaginary ills, and
mystical agony. At the same time he was gay, witty, and
capable of telling or writing the funniest nonsense, which,
after all, did make quite a lot of sense. He wrote *Dead
Souls* by fits and starts from 1836 to 1841, always in
doubt whether he was doing the right thing. He returned

to Moscow only to supervise the publication of his new work and to fight off the censors who threatened to mutilate the book and actually made numerous cuts. When finally issued in 1842, *Dead Souls* created quite a sensation. 'This is a purely national work,' wrote Belinsky. 'It derives from the depth of popular life; it is as truthful as it is merciless and patriotic; it strips the veils from reality; it is inspired by a passionate love of the true essence of the Russian world.' The social and historical implications of *Dead Souls* went again far beyond the author's expectations.

Dead Souls, which Gogol called 'a poem,' was constructed as a travel novel, a form common in the European literature of the times. Its hero, Chichikov, a plump, respectable swindler, travels a great deal in order to buy 'dead souls,' the deceased serfs for whom their noble owners must pay a tax until their death is legally established by a new census. And since Chichikov offers to take over the taxes and is even ready to add a little cash for the certificate of sale, the landowners, mystified at first, agree promptly. As a result of these unusual transactions Chichikov can show on paper that he owns thousand of 'souls' or serfs, without ever revealing that all of them are dead and buried—and this gives him an enviable social standing, the possibility of large mortgages and the hope of marrying a heiress. While pursuing his goal Chichikov meets all kinds of people—heavy-footed, dog-like squires; superficially sentimental, suave, silly noblemen who call their children Themistocles and Alcides; gossipy women, pleasant in every sense; boasting gamblers helping their fortunes by cheating; greedy misers trembling over a penny; shrewd officials for whom the law is an obstacle; sentimental babblers who are more dangerous than robbers. Chichikov visits luxurious mansions and humble crofts, dances at a governor's ball, distributes bribes to clerks in dingy offices, and works out schemes in hotel rooms. He is affable, well dressed, well fed, well liked, although nobody could say what it is that they like in him. He is non-committal, he hardly expresses any opinions, his face is so smooth as to lose its identity, he is commonplace—one of those sleek petty demons who spring from nothingness and carry about them the deadly aura of not-being, of bottomless emptiness.

On the realistic level, *Dead Souls* is a panorama of

Russian life, or to be more precise, a revelation of the quagmire of provincial stupidity and slothfulness. Gogol drew a whole gallery of portraits, and all his characters, their speech, their oddities, their contortions, and wry faces, have the double quality of satirical revelation and of disquieting reality. The characters belong to all classes of the population—from Chichikov's coachman and valet to rich country gentlemen and public prosecutors. Never before had a work of such range and artistic magnitude appeared in Russia. And the cumulative effect of all the scenes, characters, and incidents was overwhelming—was this Russia? Was it possible that this procession of freaks and knaves corresponded to reality? And thousands of readers had to own that the protagonists of *Dead Souls* were living portraits of people they all knew very well.

Realistic portraiture was, however, but a part of this multiplaned work. Every caricature could be explored in depth, and easily revealed its symbolic meaning. All of them, including Chichikov, were dead souls, or lacked any soul, and all breathed the foul smell of evil. The *exposé* of Russia's spiritual vacuum, so discouraging in its satirical sharpness, was counterbalanced only by lyrical passages, of great verbal sweep, in which Gogol gave voice to his hope in Russia's future. In the last chapter of the first volume he compared his native country to the soaring *troika;* and although he could not say whither the horses were pulling the carriage, he knew that the road was broad and bright, and the speed miraculous. And while liberal Westernizers saluted *Dead Souls* as a condemnation of Russia's social and cultural backwardness, the religious Slavophiles saw in it an act of faith in Russia's great destiny. They expected that in the second volume Gogol would make quite clear his nationalistic creed. Other poetic and symbolic motifs intermingled in this complex symphonic composition. Musical terms seem most adequate for the analysis of *Dead Souls;* its verbal unity is based mainly on its rhythmical language, the phonetic wealth of sentences, the auditory effects of allusions, repetitions, and hints. The dynamic and eccentric quality of its style, the subtle poetry of its descriptions and the brilliancy of its banter made *Dead Souls* a literary phenomenon with a strange and morbid charm. Gogol's laughter acquired in it an almost metaphysical ring. It seemed to lead to the ultimate question: is it

possible that all those twisted, disgusting mortals were
created in the image of God? This query not being an-
swered in the first volume, Gogol felt that it was his duty
to provide a catharsis; he had to resolve all the disfigure-
ments, all the monstrosities of life into a vision of goodness and harmony. This desire became his fixed idea, his
agony, his excruciating problem, and finally the cause of
his undoing.

Gogol had but a scanty knowledge of the social and
political problems of his day. He did not belong to any
ideological group of intelligentsia, and, as Tolstoy ac-
curately remarked, his shy mind was not equal to his
great intuitive artistic genius. He expressed the negative
attitude of a whole generation which languished in the
prison of Nicholas' regime, rejected its environment,
and was anxious to discuss the future of the country. But
he was not aware of what he had done, or else was quite
simply frightened by what others read into his work. He
felt the necessity for affirmation and sought support and
advice in meditation and religion. In 1842 he returned to
Rome, fell under the influence of mystical friends and
some Roman Catholic priests, and by 1847 published
Selected Passages from Correspondence with Friends, an
attempt at philosophical and political essays in which he
defended autocracy, serfdom, capital punishment, the
Greek Orthodox Church, the virtue of obedience and
conformity, and that very order of society he exposed so
completely in *The Inspector General* and *Dead Souls.*
Written in a half-Biblical, inflated style, as if he considered himself a new prophet, these articles (some of
them containing interesting passages on literature and
theatre) aroused the indignation of Belinsky, who,
almost on his death bed, wrote a fiery letter which could
not be published because of the censorship, but which attained an enormous underground circulation. Those found
in possession of it were jailed or exiled.

In the next few years Gogol tried to compose the second affirmative volume of *Dead Souls.* He planned to
show that Chichikov's swindle was unmasked and that
golden-hearted millionaires and virtuous governor's officials made the villain repent and put him on the road
to moral salvation. The poem had to end in an apotheosis,
with good triumphing over evil. But the trouble was that
Gogol was utterly incapable of drawing those saintly vi-

sions. Although his scenes of redemption were forced and lifeless, he was again highly successful in depicting cranks, gluttons, nincompoops, and other varieties in his human zoo. This exasperated him, and he wondered whether it was not the Devil himself who guided his pen. The conflict between the artist who enjoyed portraying ludicrous distortions of mankind and the religious ascetic who wanted to serve God and Morality by his writing, proved to be too much for a man undermined by fasting, illness, isolation, and horrible dreams. He burned almost everything he wrote, rewrote it again, shut himself off from the world, practised all kinds of religious discipline, went as a pilgrim to the Holy Land, and, after six years of travel, returned to Russia, only to fall under the influence of a fanatical father-confessor who convinced him that he should get rid of all his 'diabolical writings.' In 1851 Gogol obeyed and threw into the flames the second manuscript of the second volume of *Dead Souls* (only part of it, in a second copy, was preserved by friends). But this supreme sacrifice completely ruined his health, and he died from nervous exhaustion in February 1852. His funeral, attended by thousands, was a moving tribute to Russia's first great novelist.

Only in Gogol did Russian prose reach its true originality. Despite the great value of Pushkin's stories and Lermontov's novel, as well as minor works of local importance, Gogol was the first fiction writer of great stature to contribute work of lasting value to European literature. The very contradictions of this Romantic who became the head of the realistic school, of this strange humourist who looked for a religious justification for his art and combined 'the visible laughter with invisible tears,' of this jocular story-teller who found life boring and insignificant, made him an unusual figure in the world's literature. His style, colloquial and lyrical at the same time, rising from jingles and low jokes to the heights of ringing rhetoric, from the drollery of newly coined, phonetically funny words to the musical rhythm of beautifully turned passages, is one of the most unsurpassed and rich examples of Russian prose. His language, sonorous, changeable, is, in its turbulent and idiomatic flow, the opposite of the genteel and orderly tradition of a Karamzin. Later such diverse authors as writers of the soil, symbolists, and 'neo-realists' of the

Soviet era were all to claim Gogol as their teacher. His influence on his contemporaries was not less portentous. In fact all Russian writers between 1840 and 1860, perhaps with the exception of Tolstoy and the mature Turgenev, felt strongly Gogol's influence and even imitated his literary manner. No wonder that Belinsky, and later Chernyshevsky, called it 'Gogol's period in Russian letters' and ascribed the victory of the realistic school to his uncontested supremacy. But although all the textbooks still designate him as the initiator and leader of Russian realism, a great many critics call him a Romantic and admire him as a creator of dreams and fantastic visions, a mystical narrator of weird, fanciful stories.

7. From Belinsky to Herzen

The three decades of Czar Nicholas I's reign (1825-55) were oddly paradoxical. While political and social reaction froze the country, an unusual blossoming of arts and letters took place inside the gigantic and gloomy barracks into which the autocratic Russian ruler tried to change his empire. Nicholas I and his court were so frightened by the abortive uprising of the Decembrist that they suspected the 'red menace' everywhere and fought against every manifestation of liberalism, abroad as well as at home. This was the time when Russia assumed the role of 'gendarme' in Europe. The Czar intervened in France, Italy, and Austria to protect 'thrones and altars,' and sent troops to combat the revolution in Hungary. The official ideology proclaimed autocracy, Orthodox religion, the superiority of the nobility, the mute obedience of the lower classes, and the patriarchal way of life to be the firm foundations of the State. Backwardness, inertia, and ignorance, hailed as national virtues, were maintained through militarism and strong centralization. A police state organization and an army of greedy, corrupt bureaucrats, portraits of whom can be found in Gogol, Pisemsky, Saltykov, and all the realistic writers of the period, formed the backbone of the country's political regime. Red tape was everywhere, and administrative abuse could be mitigated only by bribes; serfs and common folk were mercilessly exploited and harshly treated by their superiors. Peasant conscripts had to serve in the army for twenty-five years; flogging, branding of criminals with hot irons, imprisonment, and exile were the methods of a slow and graft-ridden justice; and the whole population was ruled with barbarous cruelty. The various nationalities in the Empire were oppressed—Poles, Jews, Caucasians, and Latvians, all were maltreated, and Russian religious non-conformists and sectarians were persecuted so ruthlessly that they fled to Siberia or even emigrated to China and Canada.

The upper classes did not suffer physically like the rest of the nation, but they were harassed by spies and secret police, actively searching for 'subversive ideas' and 'un-Russian tendencies.' Nicholas I and his councillors feared and hated the 'revolutionary venom'; in their opinion it was of foreign origin, hence their suspicion of the West, the restrictive measures against travelling abroad, and the establishment of an over-all censorship. Under the pretext of fighting 'the dangerous infiltration of impiety and rebellion,' censors sifted poems, novels, textbooks, pictures, and opera scores. A contemporary compared them to 'a pack of bloodhounds unleashed on Russian literature,' and they not only were harmful, but also made such asinine decisions that the annals of the censors under Nicholas I read like a collection of schoolboy howlers. In a textbook on physics, the expression 'forces of nature' was banned as atheistic; in a cookery book the sentence 'free air is necessary for the dough' was suppressed because of its symbolic meaning. A poet who confessed that he cherished his beloved 'above everything in the world' was severely reprimanded by the censor: 'No law-abiding citizen ought to put anything above God and the Emperor.' An ethnographer was not allowed to write that sleighs were drawn by dogs in the extreme north of Russia because this fact had not been confirmed by the Police Department. Another cautious censor took a different line in banning a book that described certain faulty administrative practices: 'The very danger of the work lies in its truthfulness.'

Education fared hardly better than literature. Nicholas I had always considered universities as hot beds of liberal ideas and students and professors as potential revolutionaries, and he also spoke of the 'evil effects of learning on sons of peasants and serfs.' After the European revolutionary movements of 1848, all missions for study abroad were suspended, the chairs of Western constitutional law and philosophy were suppressed, and the teaching of such dubious subjects as psychology and logic were intrusted to theologians. Natural sciences were branded as 'sources of atheism,' and social sciences blamed for 'disseminating the contagion of radicalism.'

Russian educated society, compelled to breathe this foul atmosphere of reaction and stupidity, sought fresh air in art and philosophical speculation. Since they were denied any social and political initiative, intellectuals looked for compensation in study and creativity. This explains the paradox of the 'Golden Age' of Russian art and letters which grew under this autocratic regime of Nicholas I. 'We devoted ourselves to science, philosophy, love, military art, mysticism, in order to forget the monstrous shallowness about us,' said Alexander Herzen, himself a representative of the Golden Age and a brilliant critic of his times.

Among the many aspects of the Golden Age there was a famous poetic upsurge, led by Pushkin and Lermontov, and sustained by such poets as Tiutchev and Nekrassov, by the highly sophisticated Baratynsky, the melancholy Delvig, the mystical Odoevsky, the pagan Yazykov, and other members of the 'pleiad,' by a group of successful translators, such as Kozlov, and by 'poets of the people' such as the peasant Alexis Koltzov, and various others. This affirmation of national poetry was matched in the forties by that of prose, with Gogol's masterpieces and the high attainments of the realistic school. Such writers as Turgenev, Goncharov, Ostrovsky, Saltykov, Pisemsky, and finally Tolstoy and Dostoevsky made their literary beginnings in the forties and fifties.

The circulation of books, journalism, and literary criticism increased considerably; and periodicals, from weeklies and dailies to influential monthlies, spread all over the country. This was also the time when a national school of painting, with Konstantin Briullov, Alexander Ivanov, Orest Kiprensky, Pavel Fedotov, Alexis Venezianov, and many others, emerged, and when Russian music asserted its national traits in works by Alexander Dargomyzhsky and Michael Glinka, as well as in the pieces of minor composers. Theatre, with great actors such as Shchepkin and Mochalov, and ballet, based on traditional training, also developed magnificently.

Perhaps the most remarkable phenomenon of this extraordinary epoch was the growth of theoretical thought and the passionate interest shown by Russian intellectuals in all fields of philosophy, history, political science, and literary criticism. One could say that the political Romanticism personified by the Decembrist movement, and the literary Romanticism which found its expression in poetry, in historical narrative, in certain elements of Gogol's work, and in the popular novels of second-rate minor writers such as Bestuzhev or Zagoskin, were followed by philosophical Romanticism. The vogue of Byron, or of Scott, was soon obscured by the spell exerted by Herder, Schelling, Fichte, and later Hegel, and by the aesthetics of Schiller. German Romantic philosophers were avidly read and discussed in dozens of circles and groups which grew up in great numbers in the thirties and forties. In those circles young men paid exaggerated tribute to metaphysics and spent innumerable hours in highly abstruse debate. Turgenev described these 'knights of talk,' in *Rudin* and various novelettes.

What was typical of all these groups was the ardour with which any theoretical proposition was analysed. Young idealists of the famous circle led by Nicholas Stankevich (1813-40), who inspired his friends with the pure flame of his spiritual quest, studied Fichte and Schelling or interpreted at length a symbolic image in the second part of Goethe's *Faust* because they approached ideas, as Russians always do, on an emotional level. They did not merely study philosophy—they lived it, they meditated with passion, and they demanded from theoretical knowledge practical conclusions. They sought in a doctrine a way of life, a personal as well as a collective guide. Unlike the Germans, who indulged in abstract intellectual 'brooding' for its own sake, the Russians always looked at philosophers as teachers and drew practical implications from philosophical premises. The impact of this psychological tendency was strongly felt in the whole history of Russian intellectual life, but it had almost comical as well as serious consequences. When the pantheistic trends of German Romantic philosophy became popular among the intellectuals, young men and girls (as Herzen reported) never went for a walk in the country without seeing in it 'a manifestation of a union with nature.' One sentence fished out of some excerpts from Hegel, 'All that exists has a reason for existing,' convinced quite a number of Russian Romantics that they had to bow to autocracy, serfdom, and censorship.

The typical example of the spirit of the times is given by a man who not only reflected the mentality of his contemporaries but also exerted a tremendous influence on Russian literature. Vissarion Belinsky (born in 1811), the son of a provincial physician, was a failure in school and was turned out of Moscow University because of his poor academic record. Poverty-stricken and in ill health, this ascetic-looking young man with a frail body and an indomitable passion for ideas soon became known all over Russia as a brilliant literary critic. From 1834, when he published his first survey, until his death fifteen years later, he remained the intellectual leader of a whole generation; his interpretations of current and past literature, his essays on Pushkin, Gogol, Lermontov, and all the major and minor writers of the period, were eagerly read and discussed by the growing intelligentsia. Belinsky's intellectual and aesthetic evolution reflected the philosophical trends of his times.

At first Belinsky, a member of the Stankevich circle, was an enthusiastic supporter of Schelling's idealistic philosophy and saw in poetry and art the expression of the universal spirit, of the immortal substance of the world. Together with other dreamers he asserted the supremacy of spiritual values over the coarse reality of phenomena, and was much more interested in a poem, a sonata, or a theoretical argument than in the contemptible contingencies of this world, such as the political reality or social reform. But while climbing the beautiful heights of contemplation and wisdom, Belinsky could not help being disturbed by the laments and groans from that very vale of tears he wanted to escape. Hurt by his environment, this seeker for philosophical serenity felt more and more the necessity to define his own attitude toward Russian life. In the late thirties Hegel, introduced to Belinsky by Michael Bakunin, the future leader of international anarchism, seemed to provide a reconciliation between the problems of history and the principles of truth. If, as Hegel asserted, history was but a manifestation of the universal spirit in its progressive movement toward freedom and self-expression, then the surrounding reality of a given period was merely a phase in an inevitable evolution, and the understanding of historical necessity contained its justification. This acceptance of the existing reality as logical, in the glorious chain of Divine Reason, formed the second stage of Belinsky's intellectual quest.

After writing a few articles in which he implicitly vindicated all the evils of autocracy and slavery, arousing disputes among the young liberals, he became, however, extremely perturbed and started revising his theories. He hated those very things he tried to proclaim reasonable and justified. A sharp conflict between his moral self, which was in rebellion against the indignities of Russian life, and his philosophical approach, based on absolute values, led to a final rejection of what he then called 'Hegelian abstractions.' Belinsky came to the conclusion that the interest of the living human being ought to constitute the ground for practical philosophy and that freedom and justice, both political and social, should be the prerequisite of any historical development. Man himself creates values which serve as touchstones in his scrutiny of reality. Beauty, justice, and truth should not remain superior to life but should permeate life itself; to attain this, life must be changed. Thus the former pupil of Schelling and Hegel turned toward French humanitarian socialism and by the end of his life, grew highly influenced by positivistic tendencies. Like the majority of his contemporaries, he saw in socialism a kind of new religion, and his conversion to it had strong moral overtones. His growing interest in social and political issues was typical of the general evolution of the idealistic dreamers. In 1848, by the time of Belinsky's death, Herzen was helping the French to bring about the end of the July Monarchy; Bakunin was directing the fight at the barricades of Dresden; and Dostoevsky was attending the meetings of a secret socialist society in St. Petersburg.

In the last phase of his career Belinsky broke away from those Romantic literary critics who could be considered his predecessors (Prince Peter Viazemsky, Nicholas Polevoy, Nicholas Nadezhdin). He also departed from his early aesthetic criteria and became the exponent of sociological method. He contended that each individual writer reflects his society and his works must be analysed in connexion with the concrete reality they describe. He advanced his theory of literature as the expression of a national spirit. He also became a stout defender of realism, hailed Gogol as the head of the 'natural school,' and paid great attention to the social significance of art. 'Art for art's sake has never really existed,' he wrote not long before his death. 'Art recreates reality in its typical and most truthful aspects. Today art and literature are more than ever the expression of social problems, and that is the direction in which the Russian natural school is moving.' A radical, a Westernizer, and a patriot, he believed that Russia should seek its salvation 'in the successes of civilization, of enlightenment, of humanity.'

Part of his prodigious influence was due to his striking individuality. This thin man, marked by the stigma of tuberculosis, was a born fighter, and his friends called him 'frenzied Vissarion.' His temperament often led him to rash judgements and critical mistakes, but all his evaluations were sincere and challenging. 'My articles and my inner self are inseparable,' he said, 'and my power lies not in my talent but in my passion . . . Russian literature is my blood, my life.'

There is no doubt that the whole direction of Russian literary criticism in the nineteenth century was determined by Belinsky. He became the teacher, the law maker, and the model for future generations, and was greatly responsible for the predominance of the sociological approach. In the twentieth century his position has been assessed. Marxists saw in him a representative of 'revolutionary democracy' and their precursor; symbolists and followers of an aesthetic or religious approach to literature accused him of having 'distorted and deviated' the problem of art. There is an obvious lack of historical objectivity in all these contradictory statements. Belinsky was a mouthpiece of his times, and his shift from abstract truth and aesthetic contemplation to social awareness and socialist action was a general trend of the epoch. In the forties and fifties Russian intellectuals became more interested in history and politics than in metaphysics and aesthetics. Their attention was particularly focussed on the problem of national character and Russia's future. Two opposed currents of public opinion, the 'Westernizers' and the 'Slavophiles,' offered their diverse views on these subjects. The group of Slavophiles, led by the poet and theologian Alexis Khomiakov, one of the most important Russian religious thinkers, by the brothers Peter and Ivan Kireyevsky, and Konstantin and Ivan Aksakov, claimed that the St. Petersburg period of Russian history, which had its origin in Peter the Great's reforms, disrupted the organic unity of the Muscovite State. Only the Orthodox religion, opposed to Catholic lust for power and Protestant rationalism, has kept intact the principles of spiritual love and freedom in the masses of the Russian people, they said. The essence of Russian culture was religious, and to maintain spiritual integrity, the people had delegated temporal power to the Czars. Thus, monarchy was another essential mark of the Russian tradition. National originality, traditional ways of life, and old customs expressed the very substance of Russia, and they had to be preserved and defended against the pernicious influences of militarism, despotism, materialism, and atheism, those corrupting influences from the West which caused Russia to bow towards Europe. The West was going to be destroyed by class struggle, revolution, and the decline of religion; but Russia, personifying simplicity and solidarity (exemplified for instance in the Russian *mir* or collective cultivation of the land, and in other forms of co-operative labour) and true Christian virtue, would remain incorruptible. While the right-wing of the Slavophiles talked about the union of all Slavs under the aegis of the Russian Czar and foretold the doom of European civilization, the majority of Slavophiles sharply criticized serfdom and abuse by the autocratic regime, demanded 'full freedom of life and thought,' and dreamed of an 'Orthodox popular democracy within the framework of Monarchy' which could set an example of brotherhood and unity to the decadent West.

The Westernizers often laughed at these utopian views and attacked them as politically harmful and historically false. The discussion between Westernizers and Slavophiles took a particularly sharp turn after the publication, in 1836, of *A Philosophical Letter* by Peter Chaadaiev, a former officer in the Imperial Guards and an original religious thinker. Chaadaiev accused Russia of sterility, claimed that she had not contributed anything so far to the community of nations, and blamed her alienation from

Europe as the main cause of her backwardness. Her past was empty, her present unbearable, her future nonexistent. For him, there was only one civilization—that under Roman Law, the Catholic Church, and the Western way of life; and Russia's salvation lay in absorbing European culture and in uniting with the Catholic world.

The Westernizers refused to share Chaadaiev's religious standpoint. They simply affirmed that Russia was part of Europe and therefore belonged to Western civilization. Autocracy, serfdom, barbarous customs, and cultural and social backwardness were all of Asiatic and Byzantine origin and ought to be eradicated through the renovation of Russian institutions. While moderate Westernizers, such as Turgenev, Granovsky, Kavelin, and many educated noblemen, wanted to go on with the Europeanization of the country and the transformation of autocracy into a parliamentary regime, the radical Westernizers, with Belinsky, Bakunin, Ogarev, and Herzen, saw Westernization as a radical change in the whole structure of Russia's political and social conditions. 'All the talk about Russian humility and Orthodoxy is merely helping the reaction,' wrote Herzen. 'The future of the country lies not in the resurrection of Byzantine prejudices or pseudonational smugness but in free thought, science, individual and collective liberty, and the transformation of the social and economical order.' Herzen and his group of young noblemen, greatly impressed by the writings of French Utopian socialists, conceived of this transformation as a socialist revolution.

A widely educated man and a striking writer, Alexander Herzen (1812-70) left Russia in 1847 and, after travelling in France and Italy, settled down in London as a political *émigré*. He established a Free Press in England and printed all sorts of works banned in his homeland. His review, *The Bell,* introduced into Russia through clandestine channels, played a very important role in the political life of the fifties. More lasting and profound was the influence of Herzen's political ideas. He attempted a reconciliation of Slavophiles and Westernizers, and laid the foundations of a whole school of Russian social thought—populism. Although he affirmed his attachment to the Western concept of individual freedom and human dignity and followed European socialism, Herzen, a man of keen critical ability, was sceptical about the chances of revolution in the West. He accused Europe of pettiness, meanness, and hypocrisy, and rested all his hopes on Russia. His faith was based on what he called 'instinctive socialism' as opposed to the rational European doctrine. The existence of co-operative forms of labour and, above all, of the peasant collective community, the weakness of capitalism in the backward economy of the Empire, and the extremism of the Russian people, who always hated half-measures and maintained a primitive democracy, convinced Herzen that Russia was destined to reach social revolution directly, characteristically, and quickly, avoiding the bourgeois regimes and the clumsy parliamentarianism of the West. In fact Herzen, with Bakunin and other populists, believed that Russia's social upheaval would awaken Europe and lend her new force. 'There are only two interesting problems,' wrote Herzen in 1854, 'the social problem and the Russian problem. Basically, they are two facets of the same problem.'

Many writings of Herzen sound prophetic today; in any case most of them are extremely interesting and penetrating. In the same way as the Slavophiles, who believed that Moscow would become the Third Rome in the religious renovation of mankind, Herzen came to the conclusion that his country was called on to initiate and direct a world social revolution. It must be added that Herzen's social theories and political activities, however decisive they were for his country's radical and socialist movement, and his enormous contribution to Russian journalism should not overshadow his role as a creative writer. Author of *Past and Thought,* his brilliant and moving memoirs, of realistic novels, and of witty, ironic essays, he revealed himself a great master of prose, more than justifying Turgenev's remark that 'Herzen's style, madly irregular, fills me with delight; it is like living flesh.'

8. TURGENEV

ALL the shifting ideas and moods in mid-century Russia found their chronicler in Ivan Turgenev (1818-83), the head of a literary school, a promoter of realism at home, and an unofficial ambassador of Russian culture in Europe. This rich nobleman spent some thirty years in

France and Germany, travelling widely across the continent and the British Isles. Friend of Flaubert and Zola,
of Henry James and Berthold Auerbach, he was a familiar
and influential figure among Victorian writers and
artists between 1850 and 1880. His works, translated into
dozens of languages, were very popular in many countries, including the United States, and among the first to
reveal Russian life and literature to the Western World.

Turgenev studied at the universities of Moscow, St.
Petersburg, and Berlin with Stankevich and Bakunin, and
was a close friend of Belinsky and Herzen, without, however, becoming either a socialist or even a radical. A convinced Westernizer and a mild humanitarian liberal, he
avoided extremes in his manners as well as in his writings,
and always remained a balanced, cultured gentleman
who cherished harmony and measure as the highest attainments of art and wisdom. Those who believed that passionate brutality, emotional exuberance, and fanatical
devotion to ideas were inherent in the Russian mind found
Turgenev disappointing. In fact this amiable atheist refused to become committed to any party or creed and
never joined any political or philosophical chapel; he
maintained an equally bemused and melancholy attitude
towards the faith of his ancestors as well as towards the
changing ideologies of his contemporaries. He was one of
the very rare Russian novelists who were not *engagés*.
At the same time, even though he might have been a sen-
timentalist and a Romantic in his feelings and affections,
he kept a cool head, and as he stated himself, his mind
had a sceptical and positivistic bent.

Turgenev showed himself a great writer in his *Notes of
a Hunter,* character studies of serfs, peasants, and landowners from the point of view of a narrator, who, in his
ramblings across the fields and forests of Central Russia,
meets various people and observes episodes of rural and
provincial life. Peasant children tell fantastic stories
around a bonfire in the weird atmosphere of a summer
night (*Bezhin Meadow*); a contest between amateur
singers of popular songs deeply moves the listeners in a
shabby village inn (*The Singers*); a peasant who lives in
unison with nature and possesses the imagination of a
primitive bard is opposed by his down-to-earth, practical,
and successful friend, both typical of Russia (*Khor and
Kalynich*); a poor woman immobilized by mortal illness

finds inner resources in her naïve religion and her love of life and all the creatures of the earth (*The Living Relic*); the unhappy love affair of a peasant girl ruins all her life (*Ermolai and the Miller's Wife*)—such was the range of these plotless stories which appeared in book form in 1852 and soon became classics. For over a century they were studied in schools and were great favourites with all kind of readers. They showed serfs as human beings endowed with the same psychological conflicts and yearnings for happiness and justice as were usually attributed only to their masters.

Turgenev avoided any description of violence and brutality and did not criticize the appalling conditions of the lower classes or the insensibility of landowners, but his book was indirectly a most powerful condemnation of serfdom. His detached, objective narrative proved to be more effective than any show of indignation—the reader is infected by the author's tone and intimations, is 'tuned' indirectly, by an undertow of sympathy or aversion. Besides this hidden social message, which explains their almost sensational success at the time of publication, these stories were beautifully made, which accounts for their lasting place in literature. Their naturalness, combined with a scrupulous precision of realistic portraiture, their humanity coupled with lyricism, and their magnificent treatment of landscape, as an independent poetic device, can still captivate a modern reader. Instead of Gogol's grotesque verbal extravagance, Turgenev developed an elegantly selective language and a narrative art as delicate as watercolour, which made constant use of understatement and of poetic allusion. This style was welcomed as a novelty, especially at a period when realism expressed itself in imitations of Gogol, in Flemish truculence, or even in a certain coarseness of description. Half a century after Karamzin, the author of *Notes of a Hunter* was again excelling in ease and grace, but his smooth, almost glazed, prose, showed, in its restraint and melodious rhythm, a much higher and more refined craftsmanship. This manner prevailed in Turgenev's subsequent writings and became his trademark. Many critics, among them Dostoevsky and Tolstoy, accused him of affectation and of a morbid preoccupation with formal contrivance.

In the twentieth century, followers of a 'national tradition' questioned the validity of the Karamzin-Turgenev-

Chekhov line. They branded it as 'genteel, pale, uppish, and occidental' and opposed to it the 'full-blooded naturalness of popular parlance' as found in writers 'of the soil,' from Archpresbyter Avvakum on through Pisemsky, Leskov, and Remizov.

In his many short stories and novelettes, among them *First Love, Acya, Spring Freshets,* as well as in his six major novels, Turgenev expanded and brought to perfection his diaphanous artistry and verbal subtlety; and he also rose to the greatness of a creator of fiction who knows how to tell a fascinating tale or to make his characters convincing and alive. He was much less of a plot builder than a character painter, and all his novels are rather simple and short.

'The germ of a story with him,' wrote Henry James in 1884, 'was never an affair or a plot. That was the last thing he thought of. It was the representation of certain persons. The first form it at all appeared to him in was as the figure of one individual or a combination of individuals, whom he wished to see in action. They stood before him, definite, vivid, and he wished to know, and to show, as much as possible of their nature.' Even though this statement is right—and we know that most of his stories were based on real facts and dealt with living models—Turgenev's works have an aesthetic unity dependent on style and singleness of purpose. At the same time they all contain an underlying social idea or intent. These disparate elements make up the whole complexity of Turgenev as a writer; the reader should not be taken in by the apparently smooth surface of his prose. The novels of this poetic realist, who attached as much importance to the cadence of his sentences as his friend Flaubert, were deliberately set as pictures of changing society, as illustrations of social history.

In *Rudin* he depicted—and partly debunked—the 'talker' of the thirties and forties, the idealist who looks for comprehensive ideas, delights in philosophizing and excels in eloquence, but who fails in any practical venture and is even unable to respond to the genuine love of a charming girl. His whole existence is wasted, and his death in a foreign country is senseless. Lavretzky, the hero of Turgenev's next novel, *A Nest of Gentlefolk* (1859), does not resemble the loquacious and superficial Rudin, but he fares not much better: even though he is serious, has strong feelings, and falls deeply in love with Liza Kalitina, he lacks a sense of reality, is estranged from his Russian surroundings and is unprepared for life. Both are 'superfluous men.' Liza, one of Turgenev's most poetic figures, is stronger than Lavretzky (Turgenev's women are always stronger than his men) and is of a profoundly religious nature; but the integrity of her faith and the purity of her mind make her reject any earthly compromise. She cannot build her happiness at the expense of others, and flees from the harsh realities of the world into a convent; her existence is as useless at that of her lover or of Rudin.

Although secondary characters in *On the Eve* (1860) add to the series of weak and unsuccessful intellectuals, two new figures announce an imminent psychological and social change. Insarov, whom Turgenev made a Bulgarian, probably to intimate that he was not typical of Russia, embodied energy, will power, and singleness of purpose. He awakens love and devotion in Elena, another strong-willed girl resolved to live up to her ideals of freedom and activity. In a general atmosphere of expectation, she heralds the advent of feminine emancipation and of a new time.

In *Fathers and Sons* (1862), written after the abolition of serfdom, this new time had finally come. Bazarov, the hero of the novel, grandson of a deacon and son of a poor country surgeon, has nothing of the defects of the superfluous men. He is down to earth and matter of fact, he knows and gets what he wants, and his logical mind is not obscured by illusion and prejudice. A rationalist, he personifies the revolt of the practical sixties against the sterile eloquence and the quixotic nonsense of aesthetes and idealists. For him nature is not a temple but a workshop; he hails usefulness and action, effort and attainment. He belongs to a new social group of intellectuals who have risen from lower orders, and his clash with idealistic noblemen assumes the character of a class struggle; but he also represents a new psychological type, even though, in his brutal frankness, in his hatred of conventions and frills, in his devotion to the new ideologies of 'deeds against words,' he shows himself to be as Russian as his noble and useless counterpart.

Fathers and Sons, probably Turgenev's most remarkable novel and certainly his best in plot, variety of char-

acters, structure, and dramatic unity, provoked a sensational upheaval. Some of the young nonconformists accepted with joy the term 'nihilists,' coined by the writer;
others accused him of 'slandering the new generation' and
saw in the word a sneering label, and in Bazarov a caricature. The conservatives, on the other hand, found him too
lenient toward youth and 'a flunkey of the revolutionaries.'
Radicals discovered in the premature death of Bazarov a
proof of Turgenev's lack of faith in Russia: did he not
want to intimate that strong positive men like Bazarov
were destined to perish in the country's dark ignorance?
In vain did Turgenev invoke his realistic method and
claim that objectivity was his aim: 'to reproduce truth,
the very reality of life, is the highest happiness for the
writer,' he stated, 'even if that truth does not coincide
with his own sympathies.' Even the most obvious meaning of the novel—the eternal conflict between age and
youth, each holding to its own truth, the clash of two generations, was forgotten in the heat of the controversy.

Turgenev felt so depressed by the insults and injustice
of public discussion that he remained silent for several
years. Only in 1867 did he publish *Smoke,* a novel with
a slender plot in which Russian reactionaries, Slavophiles, Westernizers, and Liberals, meet in Baden-Baden
and exchange opinions about contemporary issues. The
bitter tone of this work and its pessimistic conclusions—
everything in Russia is as unstable and worthless as smoke
—did not help to reconcile Turgenev with his readers;
and his last long narrative, *The Virgin Soil,* devoted to
the populist movement of the seventies, did not appear
until ten years later (1877). Despite some good portraiture, it is the least successful of his novels.

It has often been said that Turgenev's main theme was
the problem of the superfluous man and that his gallery of
Russian types represented the intelligentsia and the nobility between 1840 and 1870. But this is only partly true.
Turgenev's topics and manner, including his interest in
weak men and strong women, are not sociological, but
have deep roots in his personality. He was himself rather
weak, and akin to his unhappy heroes. After a gloomy
childhood with a despotic and frustrated mother, Turgenev spent a difficult youth and, at the age of twenty-
five, met Pauline Viardot Garcia, the famous singer, whom
he loved and for whom he suffered all his life. This tall

(over six foot three) imposing man had a thin, feminine voice which did not fit his athletic build; and he was ridden by many contradictions and complexes. He was wealthy, he became a famous writer, he could arrange his existence as he pleased; yet his work reflects melancholy and dissatisfaction. All his novels end with renunciation and death, the latter often violent. Most of his stories describe failures or accidents, fiascos or blunders. He never shows any fulfilment; he is at his best only when dealing with expectations of flesh and soul, with wistfulness in love, with the first stirrings of desires, which, however, always remain unrealized.

In *Senilia,* his most revealing collection of poems in prose, as well as in those stories with slightly mystical undertones (*A Trip to Polessie, Phantoms, Clara Milich*), he stated that there could be no true attainment on earth, that life was always vanquished by annihilation, that the interminable law of destruction reigned over the universe, and that all our efforts were absurd. This sense of futility and doom, this awareness of the vanity of all things and of the inevitable flight of time are hidden under his glorification of youth, spring, and love, as the most beautiful affirmation of life. Here again, one has the feeling that Turgenev stuck to this glorification in the most poetic pages of his work only in order to forget death and 'the horror of eternity.'

In one of his letters to Pauline Viardot, he writes: 'I cannot stand the empty skies, but I adore life, its reality, its whims, its accidents, its rites, its swiftly passing beauty.' His was not an easy love, because he regretted passing beauty and could not forget the empty skies in the palpable reality of human affairs. He was very sensitive to all the charms and guiles of existence, but he enjoyed them with an incurable sadness. He chose to render in his writings all those momentary affirmations of vitality in which man forgets his destiny. His best pages describe the dreams and aspirations of youth, the hopes for happiness, and particularly the first blossoming of love or the bliss of art, mostly of music, the intoxication of idealistic struggle. Youth, spring, charming women who open their hearts to the tremulous voices of love—these were his favourite visions, darkened in later years by the shadow of annihilation.

Whatever critics may think about his historical value

and his role as a realist, it is his lyrical gift and his conception of a work of art as an orderly arrangement of emotional shadings, that make Turgenev one of the most important Russian, and perhaps European, prose writers of the nineteenth century.

9. GONCHAROV AND OSTROVSKY

TURGENEV was not alone in his concern with the superfluous man—in one way or another this problem was raised in almost every realistic work of the fifties; and it was dealt with masterfully in the novels of Goncharov, a great realist, and Turgenev's rival and enemy.

Ivan Goncharov (1812-91) was born in a small town on the Volga river and raised on a patriarchal estate where masters lounged in idleness while hosts of serfs and peasants attended to their whims. He received a summary education and at the age of twenty-two entered government service. During the thirty-three years of his career he occupied varied posts, including that of a censor, and rose steadily in the administrative hierarchy. A mild conservative and a confirmed bachelor, he led an orderly, monotonous existence, interrupted but once, in 1856, by a trip around the world, which he described in his *Frigate Pallas*. But this stout, well-fed gentleman with heavy whiskers and slow dignified manners, the image of the perfect bureaucrat, was a writer. He sought happiness and compensation in depicting imaginary heroes who were his best and worst selves, and he produced three novels. He wrote them patiently, painfully; it took him ten years (1849-59) to complete *Oblomov* and another ten to finish *The Precipice* (1859-69).

He was thirty-five when he published his first novel, *A Common Story,* which was acclaimed by the critics and the public as a model of naturalistic portraiture. The hero of this autobiographical work, Alexander Aduev, is a provincial young idealist who writes bad verse and dreams of great passions, but who is taught a harsh lesson by his Uncle Peter, a St. Petersburg official and a rational positivist. With this painful eye-opening (which in parts can be compared to Balzac's *Lost Illusions* and Flaubert's *Sentimental Education*), Aduev renounces all

his Romantic illusions. He ends up a second-rate governmental clerk and is about to marry some insignificant
girl with plenty of money.

Goncharov's major work, the monumental *Oblomov*,
also has an autobiographical flavour. Whereas *A Common
Story* is an *exposé* of shallow idealism and false romanticism, *Oblomov* is a debunking of the superfluous man.
The protagonist of this bulky novel is, like his creator,
raised on a Volga estate in an atmosphere of laziness and
plenty and is pampered and protected from reality, while
serfs toil and moil for him. In due time he enters the University of St. Petersburg and shares in the idealistic strivings of his generation. He is intelligent and kind-hearted
but too soft and lazy to pursue any of the hazy projects
born in his imagination. He prefers to daydream while
lounging on his sofa. This paralysis of will is rooted in
his ineradicable contempt for action: he firmly believes
that inactivity is a symbol of social superiority and that
work is a curse. His love for Olga provokes a momentary
recovery but ends in an impasse, because the young girl
has brains and a desire for action, and this proves to be
too much of a disturbance for Oblomov and tires him
out. She finally marries Oblomov's school-mate, the
methodical German Stolz, who has tried unsuccessfully
to rouse his friend and to make him change the deadly
routine of idleness. Oblomov ends his days in the house
of the prosaic and ignorant widow Agatha. She cooks fat
meals for him and gives him the illusion of a return to
childhood, into the undisturbed beatitude of food, sleep,
and relaxation.

While other superfluous men in Russian literature were
not deprived of their slight Romantic halo, Oblomov is
presented with the merciless clarity of a clinical case. The
critic, Nicholas Dobroliubov, wrote in his famous article
'What is Oblomovism?' that Oblomov's disease came
about through serfdom and that all his noble predecessors
—from Oneghin down to Rudin—were infected by the
same virus. Oblomovism was the by-product of slave labour and backwardness. The upper classes considered
work a social disgrace, and inefficiency as a mark of nobility. Oblomovism therefore was a social phenomenon.
Some fifty years later, twentieth-century critics questioned whether Oblomov was simply a victim of environment. They saw in Oblomovism not only the expression of

a psychological reluctance to accept reality, a complex of immaturity with a subsequent manifestation of infantilism, but also a sign of Oriental fatalism. Oblomov's escape from life was determined by his underlying belief in the superiority of contemplation over action. He did not want to be an agent in the process of history, and like many Russians, he denied any value to individual intervention in current events. His inefficiency, his laissez-faire were akin to the Asiatic glorification of inactivity, and there was a little of Oblomov in every Russian, they said.

Whatever the interpretation of Oblomovism, the novel made a great impression in the sixties and was later ranked with the greatest works of Russian fiction. Gogol's sparkling metaphorical prose or Turgenev's compact, highly nuanced novels, are of a totally different texture from Goncharov's circumstantial narrative, with its cumulative copiousness of concrete detail. Goncharov is in no hurry. Time, in fact, is his ally and one of his literary devices. He conveys its flow to the reader; patiently, repetitiously, he makes his point, reproduces verbatim long dialogues, shows his hero from every angle, does not forget to mention inanimate objects, the minutiae of environment, food, clothes, furniture, so that his vision of life is exhaustive, or seems so, and in any case creates a perfect illusion of reality. His heavy procrastinating pace is not deprived of its own majesty. The power of this most Flemish of Russian masters lies not in plot or dramatic action (both are reduced to a strict minimum), but in character study and in almost naturalistic representation of surroundings. As a Russian critic put it, his placid manner resembled 'a room with easy chairs, heavy draperies, and soft carpets, where footsteps are muffled and the discordant notes of passion are muted.'

Unlike the naturalists, however, Goncharov did interrupt his narrative with generalizations and personal remarks. Not satisfied with his success as a faithful painter of Russian reality, he wanted to become a moralist and a teacher, and he never missed an opportunity for expressing a moral judgement. As long as he remained within the bounds of common sense and indulgent casual humour, he did well, but whenever he attempted to interpret the ideas and social currents of his times and tried to censure the progressive movement, he did not rise above a middle-of-the-road, middle-class mentality. This is most visible in his last novel, *The Precipice,* a lengthy chronicle of the sixties. It contains delightful descriptions of a small estate in the Volga region and excellent character studies of its owner, the old grandmother Berezhkova, of her niece Marfinka, a charming 'simple hearted' youngster, and of Raisky, a dilettante painter, an aesthete and a member of the superfluous man caste. Much weaker are the portraits of Vera, the beautiful heroine, and of her seducer, the nihilist Mark Volokhov. Their crippled love-affair was supposed to prove the failure of the new generation and the falsity of new ideas. After her 'fault' Vera returns to the 'old truth' of her ancestors and accepts the love of the practical and virtuous Tushin, and Grandmother Berezhkova rises to become the symbolic incarnation of Russia. The last part of the novel, where Goncharov acts as a *raisonneur,* is pretentious and vapid, and artistically unconvincing. All his positive heroes, Aduev's uncle, Stolz, Tushin, are successful business men and models of respectability, and Goncharov welcomed them as the opposite of the degenerated scions of idle nobility, or the Godless revolutionaries; but these embodiments of bourgeois conservatism failed to enthral Russian readers.

It was a fact that the bourgeoisie and the middle class were asserting themselves in the sixties, but their rise was a complex social phenomenon, partly connected with the peculiarities of certain previously formed economic and social groups. One of them—the most influential and the most colourful—was the class of Russian merchants, which their chronicler, Alexander Ostrovsky, discovered and introduced into Russian literature. Son of a poor government employee, Alexander Ostrovsky (1823-86) himself became a clerk in Moscow's Court of Equity and Court of Commerce, where he found ample opportunities to study the 'across-the-river-folk' as the bearded merchants of the city were called because of the location of their old-fashioned houses. Ostrovsky's subsequent activity as a pettifogger, versed in the intricacies of law suits and feuds among the merchants, added to his wealth of information. Trips across the Volga region expanded his knowledge of the Russian middle-class.

He portrayed in his comedies this peculiar world of despotic heads of family who ruled like dictators at home and in their shops, of ignorant wives and resigned sons and daughters—a whole section of Russian life which revealed such abuse, ignorance, and coarseness that Dobroliubov called it 'the realm of darkness.' One of Ostrovsky's main heroes was the 'samodur' or wilful stubborn man, a petty tyrant. 'When he stamps his foot, the whole household has to get down on its knees,' says one of Ostrovsky's protagonists. When Bolshov, the merchant in *It's All in the Family,* decides to marry off his daughter, he dismisses all the objections of the fellow he had chosen as his future son-in-law—'Isn't she my daughter? I made her, I can do whatever I please with her.' The samodur asserts his authority and ownership by violence —shouting, slapping, flogging—but he also reverts to 'smart tricks,' including cheating, particularly in money matters. Most of these dramas of the 'realm of darkness' revolve around property and marriage, and mostly concern young girls being disposed of by their fathers as saleable goods.

Ostrovsky's world of merchants, clerks, small tradesmen, and little townsfolk, with their superstitions, ignorance, and the medieval pattern of their family life, was very close to the patriarchal peasantry from which it had sprung and was therefore illustrative not only of the merchant class but of various other strata of Russian society. The Slavophiles, with whom Ostrovsky has been associated at the beginning of his career, claimed that all his heroes, even the most repulsive ones, had hidden virtues. The lack of moderation, the animal spirits, and even the wilfulness of some of them were interpreted as sheer expressions of physical strength. In Liubim Tortzov *(Poverty No Disgrace),* the wastrel who succeeds in making his rich samodur brother repentant, the Slavophiles saw the embodiment of the 'Russian Soul,' expansive, irrational, kind, and human even in the slough of drunkenness. Ostrovsky, however, parted company with the Slavophiles in the sixties. A convinced realist, he could never be dogmatic or 'arrange facts' for the sake of an abstraction. The idealization of a Liubim Tortzov could not justify the evils of his surroundings. Ostrovsky's comedies and dramas were so openly critical of Russian conditions that some of them were banned by the authorities.

His most popular play, *The Thunderstorm* (1860), which Dobroliubov called 'a sunbeam in the realm of darkness,' was far from being optimistic. Its heroine,

Katerina, a poetically religious young woman, cannot stand the despotic rule of Kabanova, her mother-in-law, and the dullness of her weak husband. During the absence of the latter she has an affair with Boris, an attractive youth maltreated in his turn by his uncle, the samodur Dikoi. Tormented by her conscience, her nerves set on edge by a thunderstorm, Katerina makes a public confession of what she considers a mortal sin. Her life then is made so miserable by Kabanova and the hypocritical community that she goes mad with despair and commits suicide, while her lover is packed away to Siberia. It is questionable whether this story could be called a 'sunbeam' and whether Katerina, as well as men like her lover or Kuligin, a self-taught inventor, who believes in education and science, did announce the imminent decline of the samodur's power.

Ostrovsky did not limit himself to the portraiture of a single class, even though his most popular plays such as *Poverty No Disgrace, Even the Wise Stumble, It's All in the Family, The Thunderstorm,* and many others, dealt with the merchants of a certain kind and type. He exposed the bureaucrats in *Profitable Business* and the declining nobility in *Wild Money* or *Without Dowry,* and devoted some plays to provincial actors (*The Forest* and *Talents and Suitors* are the best of them). In the seventies he tried his hand at historical and folklore fantasies; among the latter his *Snow Maiden* inspired the opera by Rimsky-Korsakov.

In all his prolific production (he wrote and adapted forty-seven plays) Ostrovsky revealed himself a major exponent of 'critical realism,' which reigned in Russian literature after Gogol. In the fifties and sixties, and for long afterwards, to represent reality also meant to expose the evils of society and the defects of men. In Goncharov the critical intent was obvious, and so it was in Ostrovsky. One can say that criticism of surroundings made a link between all Russian realists—it forms one of the most characteristic features of Russian fiction of the last two centuries.

Ostrovsky did in the theatre what Gogol, Goncharov, and Turgenev accomplished in fiction. Instead of the melodramas and French farces which crowded the stage in his time, he introduced realistic comedies and dramas with Russian characters and simple plots rooted in the manners and events of national life. Before him, Russian theatres had produced two plays by Fonvizin and Griboyedov, Gogol's *Inspector General,* the rarely produced play *The Wedding,* and Turgenev's plays, among which only *A Month in the Country* survived. Ostrovsky offered a series of excellent plays with a great variety of themes and types. He was actually the founder of Russian repertory, and he remained its unchallenged ruler for over a century. Many critics wondered what would happen to Ostrovsky's plays when grain dealers, wilful merchants, matchmakers, and corrupt middlemen disappeared from Russian life. Was not Ostrovsky a regional period writer whose elementary characters lacked universality? Facts, however, did not seem to confirm this negative statement. Ostrovsky weathered wars and revolutions, and his popularity in Russia is greater in the twentieth century than in the nineteenth century. During the theatrical season of 1870 his plays were presented daily in four or five theatres; in 1912, in seven or eight; and in 1940 twenty-eight of Ostrovsky's plays were produced daily in the U.S.S.R.

There are various factors which made his literary heritage so lasting. Among other things, Ostrovsky is a truly national writer—in his dialogues which preserve all the intonations and sonority of colloquial speech (so difficult for translation), in his characters who represent the cross section of the Russian land. They are far away from the tense morbidity of Dostoevsky's heroes, from the melancholic gentleness of Turgenev's noblemen, from the heavy earthiness of Goncharov's idlers, or from the moral vulnerability of Tolstoy's seekers after God. Their follies or vices have nothing mysterious about them. They are average, matter-of-fact men and women, and their struggle for freedom and happiness against the weight of environment and the abuse they suffer at the hands of little dictators, is as familiar under the Soviets as it was under the Czars. Despite his highly critical attitude towards life and people, Ostrovsky's work is basically optimistic and wholesome. There is in it a faith in human values, an acceptance of this world which is akin to that very affirmation of life we find in Pushkin, in Tolstoy, and even in Goncharov. And this trait is no less typically Russian than the nostalgia of Chekhovian weaklings or the masochistic frenzy of Dostoevsky's rebels. Finally, Ostrovsky's warmth towards all the victims of the samodurs, the kind-

liness with which he presents the main themes of his plays
—the conflict between the wilful and the submissive,
the rich and the poor, old age and youth, tradition and
innovation—derive from that sense of pity, that Christian sympathy for the downtrodden that the West believed to be an essential feature of Russian fiction.

It must be added that Ostrovsky avoids sentimentality
(except for some 'happy endings' often imposed upon
him by stupid censors), that his plays are solidly constructed, with simple plots and a consistent development
of action which, except for a few abrupt *dénouements,*
gives the impression of great naturalness. It does not
lapse, however, into photographic imitation: Ostrovsky
the realist organized his material with a sense of theatre
which made him not only a great chronicler of Russian
life but also a great playwright.

10. FROM NIHILISTS
TO REVOLUTIONARIES

THE reign of Nicholas I ended with the collapse of an
illusion—the unhappy Crimean war of 1854-55 bared all
the technical and political ills of a regime which had previously boasted of its strength. Slavophiles, as well as
Westernizers, bitterly resented military defeat accompanied by a loss of prestige in Europe and in the Middle
East. The new czar, Alexander II, lacked firmness. He
could not break away from his reactionary environment
or destroy the wall erected by the court between the
throne and the country; but he became aware of the necessity for reforms and was ready to grant them, without, however, going too far. This ambivalence caused all
the contradictions in his policy and had fateful consequences; but at the beginning of Alexander II's reign his
liberal tendencies prevailed, and under the pressure of
public opinion the formidable problem of serfdom, the
greatest issue in Russian life, was finally solved. In 1861
the Czar's decree announcing its abolition set free millions
of peasants, who were granted land allotments with the
retention of *mir,* the collective rural community (this was
partly due to Slavophile influence). The peasants, however, had to pay the price of their freedom—indemnities
to landowners on an instalment basis. By 1903 the sum

paid by Russian peasants (with poll taxes and accrued interest) rose to over a billion gold dollars.

The liberation of the serfs released new economic forces and necessitated readjustments in the whole fabric of the State. Measures taken by the government changed the face of the country, and the sixties were called the 'era of great reforms.' The introduction of Zemstwo, local self-government, which, despite its limited functions and nondemocratic structure, played a great role in Russia's social development; the establishment of universal military training (with certain exemptions for privileged classes); the revision of the Judicial Code, followed by public hearings, trial by jury, and the abolition of corporal punishment (retained, however, for peasants and Siberian exiles); relaxation of censorship, expansion of education based on a new school system, widening of academic freedom in universities, annulment of restrictions in the press and book trade—these and many other improvements stirred every social group. Even though the basic relationship between the ruling group and the rest of the country remained untouched and autocracy maintained its absolute 'divine' rights, rejecting the idea of a parliamentary regime, still, the impact of the transformation was momentous; and it was within the social, economic, and political framework created in the sixties that Russia lived and grew until the first revolution of 1905.

The liberation of the serfs, the rise of the bourgeoisie, and the economic progress of the lower middle-class strongly affected educated society. The Romantic military nobleman of the twenties and the idealistic landowner or civil servant of the forties were replaced by the intellectual who hailed practicality and action. The nobility kept losing its exclusive cultural position; and *rasnochintsy,* scions of various social groups, mostly of the lower classes, and all with new intellectual attitudes, rose to important positions in arts, letters, and science. The *rasnochintsy* sustained the 'natural school' in literature and applauded Ostrovsky's plays; they promoted realism in painting and music and greatly contributed to the development of the natural sciences; in fact, they dominated the whole artistic and moral atmosphere of the period.

Their rationalism and social radicalism found its expression in the works by Nicholas Chernyshevsky (1828-

89), son of a priest, economist, and literary critic. His articles in *The Contemporary,* a most influential monthly, attacked sentimentalism and Utopianism, and interpreted current literary production, poetry and prose alike, as determined by social and material environment. The authorities, disturbed by the growing popularity of this socialist and his influence on the youth, arrested Chernyshevsky, accused him of plotting against the security of the State, and despite scanty legal evidence, sentenced him to hard labour. After twenty-one years of Siberian exile, he was allowed to return to Russia; but he died a few years later, a broken man. During his lifetime his name was banned from the Russian press; he was usually called the 'author of *Essays on the Gogol Period in Russian Literature,*' the title of his important series of articles on Gogol, in which he analysed the salient features of the 'natural school' and announced the victory of realism in Russian letters.

The radical youth, however, mentioned him in their songs as the author of *What Is to Be Done?* Chernyshevsky wrote this famous novel while imprisoned in the St. Peter and Paul Fortress in St. Petersburg, and his heroes such as Vera Pavlovna, the new emancipated woman, or Kirsanov, the rationalist physician, served as models for young nihilists and radicals. Even more popular and impressive seemed to them the third protagonist of this fictional social manifesto, the young nobleman Rakhmetov, who renounces all the pleasures of the earth in order to serve the cause. Even though he is utterly unbelievable and poorly depicted, he symbolized the dreams of the young and inflamed their imagination. They saw in his monastic severity and intransigent extremism a perfect counterpart to the 'superfluous man.' However curious it might seem, this bloodless figure initiated a series of equally artificial images which abounded in Soviet fiction between 1930 and 1959, when dozens of energetic and virtuous party secretaries were themselves moulded on Rakhmetov.

In the twentieth century Chernyshevsky was often considered as a forerunner of communist aesthetics. He not only affirmed the supremacy of life over art, considering literary works solely as reflections of social phenomena, but also made an attempt at building a theoretical basis for the strictly sociological method he employs in his

dry, pedestrian critical essays. His pupil, Nicholas Dobroliubov (1836-61), also a priest's son and a former student
in a theological seminary, was a much better writer. Even
though he never departed from the strictures of sociological methods, his articles on Turgenev, Goncharov, and
Ostrovsky went beyond the analysis of ideas and social
conditions. The tone of his and Chernyshevsky's essays,
in which art was interpreted as a direct representation of
reality, determined Russian literary criticism for years to
come. Dobroliubov identified literature with social service and demanded from writers a conscientious effort at
reforming society. The work of art was to him a source of
energy and an expression of ideas. Its contents actually
shaped its form. For a generation which was more interested in economics and natural science than in history
and philosophy, such statements appeared very logical
and attractive. Young men and women of the sixties always
wanted to deal with 'facts' and looked with contempt at
'castles in the air.'

Their aspirations were formulated in a most challenging way by the 'enfant terrible' of the period, Dimitri
Pisarev (1840-68), a young nobleman who possessed
the witty pen of a first-rate journalist and polemicist. Like
Dobroliubov's, his life was short (he died at the age of
twenty-eight, probably by committing suicide, but he
was already well known at twenty-two. Each of his articles
made a sensation—he seemed to be the exact voice of
his contemporaries, uttering what they thought and
wished to say. First of all, he discarded sentimentalism,
platonic love, idealism, and poetic dreams as 'sheer drivel,'
as a sign of weakness. 'Whatever detracts us from our
main tasks—education, scientific development, material,
and social progress—is useless and therefore obnoxious'
—this statement by Pisarev became gospel to the young.
They agreed heartily when he said that money spent on
ballet, theatre, and books of poetry should be used for
building railroads. Pisarev attacked Pushkin's works as
'something that merely helped the drones to kill time.'
Although he enjoyed making such statements ('a pair of
boots is more useful than a Shakespeare play') in order
to 'tease the philistine,' his readers took him most seriously. Thousands of them were rallying under the banner of
'positive thinking and no nonsense.'

Chernyshevsky and Dobroliubov were mainly concerned

with large economic and social issues and emphasized the problems of history and political change. Pisarev was chiefly interested in the individual and advised his followers to rely on experimental knowledge as the 'only safe ground for a truly rational outlook on nature, man, and society.' He denied all authority, moral or literary, and spoke of independence of judgement, freedom, and utility as the supreme guiding principles for every self-respecting person. The nihilists were particularly sensitive to these sermons. Their revolt began within their family—they questioned paternal authority, challenged social conventions and good manners, broke away from homes, and adopted brusque, often coarse ways of speech and behaviour. A great many of them came from the nobility, and their defiance of the accepted code was simply a reaction against the stuffiness of 'gentlefolk nests' and the idealistic aestheticism of their elders. It was precisely among the upper classes that the term 'nihilism' acquired its derogatory meaning and became the symbol of anarchy and debauchery.

Horrified mothers and fathers saw girls cut their hair, smoke cigarettes and—the sign of utter perdition—treat males as equals, while boys wore boots and Russian blouses, grew long whiskers, talked loudly without mincing their words and spoke of religion as 'a lot of trash.' The new fashion called for the strangest kind of attire ('we have no time for such trifles as coiffeurs, frills, and cosmetics'), and it certainly was the unusual exterior of the nihilists that struck the imagination of their less eccentric contemporaries. A bespectacled student with bobbed hair (if female) and with long hair (if male) represented the nihilist in the eyes of polite society; but for the authorities, nihilist meant 'an enemy of the established order.' In truth, nihilism was initially non-political —under its disguise of rudeness and exaggeration lay a desire for work and practical action. It was egotistical and secular. Thousands of its followers went into all sorts of professions, contributed to the building of railroads and schools, or studied abroad; and the movement for feminine emancipation, originated in nihilist circles, spread far and wide throughout Russia and forced the government to establish various institutions of higher learning for women.

In the early sixties nihilism remained within the bounds

of a purely intellectual fad. Its followers sympathized with
the socialist and radical trend of their times but were not
politically minded. The change came when their attempts
at practical activity clashed with police authority and
when they were confronted with the actual conditions of
Russian life. The government looked at them with suspicion and hampered their efforts; and their discontent
coincided with that in liberal and radical circles, when expectations of a basic change in Russia's regime and in a
'crowning of reforms' were not fulfilled. The Czar, swayed
by members of the landed aristocracy and old bureaucrats, refused to yield to the idea of a parliamentary
monarchy and kept intact his autocratic rule. Besides,
even after the reforms, the whole structure of Russian
society was most discriminatory, and only classes privileged by birth (aristocracy and nobility), function (bureaucracy and clergy), wealth (landed proprietors and
'Merchants of the First Guild'), or education (university
graduates), fully enjoyed civic rights. The peasants, the
lower middle-class, the artisans, the workers, the common
folk at the base of the social pyramid, were treated as
'scum of the earth' and were subject to oppression, exploitation, and abuse. The young radicals did not hesitate
to express their feelings in revolutionary action, and in
1866 Karakozov, a university student, fired at the Czar.
After his execution, authorities adopted an iron-handed
policy which, instead of inspiring fear, heightened the
tension. The nihilists, who before were mainly interested
in their personal rebellion, became involved in political
conspiracy. Numerous underground circles in which the
writings of Herzen and Chernyshevsky, as well as those
of Western economists and sociologists were discussed,
became sources of revolutionary propaganda.

By the beginning of the seventies, the transformation
was complete. While educated society, chiefly youth, was
seething with clandestine left-wing agitation, the influence
of Dobroliubov, Pisarev, and other 'men of the sixties'
(such as Zaitzev and Tkachev) was supplanted by that
of the exponents of socialism. The intellectual leadership
went to Peter Lavrov (1823-1900), a scholarly revolutionary and a founder of populism, and to Michael
Bakunin (1814-76), whose rivalry with Marx shook the
first International. Both escaped from Siberia to the West
and spent their lives in Europe as *émigrés*. Their works

were smuggled into Russia through numerous underground channels.

The 'thinking realists,' as Pisarev called Bazarov's pupils, quickly learned their bitter lesson. The liberated serf was far from being happy, the common people were suffering from administrative abuse and economic subjection, ignorance and misery reigned in villages and provincial towns, Russia was still a feudal semi-barbaric state in spite of the magnificent façade of its capital and few big cities, and the only salvation lay in the overthrow of the autocratic regime and in its replacement by a collectivistic society.

This vision of socialist revolution was accompanied by the populist myth. Young intellectuals found their ideal in the idea of the Russian people, who, in their dreams, became not only victims of misery and oppression but also paragons of kindness and of instinctive socialist virtue. The Slavophiles hailed national traditions and believed that Russia was blessed by the grace of true religion; her historical destiny was to fulfill the promise of Christian love and to establish the Kingdom of God on earth. The populists asserted that the Russian people were collectivistic at heart and in custom and that their calling was to achieve socialism. They also hoped that if the good peasants were awakened by means of propaganda, they would come naturally to the awareness of their needs and possibilities and would build the perfect society.

Peter Lavrov, the author of *Historical Letters,* an epoch-making book which shaped the mentality of the seventies, claimed that every educated man had obligations towards the popular masses which, by their toil, made possible all achievement in art and thought. In fact, the whole temple of culture, he said, was built on foundations laid by manual labour. Millions suffered, hungered, and died to provide leisure for the upper classes which created the fine flowers of civilization. It was morally imperative to pay one's debt to the people by founding a social order which would offer culture and welfare to all instead of to a privileged minority. Socialism represented such an order, and those who hastened its advent were rendering true service to Russia and to mankind.

The moral overtones of this blend of socialist ideas with Russian messianistic utopianism, greatly appealed to the 'repented nobleman,' a fairly frequent type in the seventies, who, wishing to atone for his privileges of birth and education, was attracted by the idea of social service, which was at the same time a sacrifice and a penitence. The *rasnochintsy* who came from the lower classes, did not need such moral justification, but they also felt the emotional beauty of renunciation and the enchantment of populist faith. For many energetic young men and women who called themselves nihilists but were idealists in disguise, populism offered an outlet for heroic and altruistic aspiration.

While Lavrov recommended the method of pacific propaganda, which, he trusted, would spread like wildfire, Bakunin suggested direct action. He contended that the Russian people had hidden wells of revolutionary passion, and that uprisings, insurrections, and open clashes with Czarist authorities would serve as a concrete lesson in revolution to the masses and would actually undermine autocratic rule.

At the beginning of the seventies, Lavrov's ideas prevailed, and the populists passed from theoretical discussion to practical action. They planned a 'crusade to the people' which soon involved thousands of young idealists of both sexes, most of them belonging to the landed nobility and the aristocracy. They went to the villages as carpenters, artisans, and nurses, and to factories as simple workers, in order to live the same life as the toilers of Russia. Soon, however, they came to the realization that their disjointed efforts were a waste of energy. Peasants and workers looked with hostility at these strange apostles of equality, and police had no difficulty in rounding up all the messengers of the new faith. By 1875 it became evident that 'going to the people' required a planned preparation. A clandestine party, 'Land and Freedom,' the first of its kind in Russia, took over the leadership of the movement and launched the second wave of the crusade. It was again smashed, mainly on account of repressive measures adopted by the government. Hundreds of populists were tried and sentenced to prison and hard labour, while thousands were sent to prison without trial. The hope that Russia could jump from Czarism into a realm of socialism without passing through Western parliamentary democracy seemed to diminish every day. The so-called economists (Marx's *Capital* was translated into Russian in 1872) still believed that political freedom was a minor issue compared to the basic problem of capitalism, but the majority of the populists came to the conclusion that the struggle for political rights had priority over everything else. We must achieve a democratic regime in Russia, they argued, as a prerequisite for the further development of socialism.

The growing reaction in the country and the stiffening of governmental counter-attack, as well as the 1877-78 war for the liberation of Balkan Slavs, provoked a heightening of the revolutionary mood among the intellectuals. The peaceful propagandist gave ground to the grim terrorist. In 1879 the new 'Party of the Popular Will' succeeded the battered 'Land and Freedom.' This centralized conspiracy organization asserted that a democratic regime sanctioned by the freely expressed will of the people was the immediate aim of the Party, and that the struggle against the ruthless autocracy was an armed conflict, in which the Party had the right to use violence. The Central Committee of the Party was a group of self-sacrificing, idealistically minded men and women who set to work with enthusiasm and absolute devotion. Terrorists and martyrs at the same time, they gave numerous examples of courage and moral stamina in their desperate struggle against the all-powerful government. They were determined to kill because they were ready to die. Set as a monastic order, the Central Committee shook Russia with bomb explosions, sensational escapes from prison, and attempts on the life of the Czar and his high functionaries. Gallows, firing squads, hard labour, and all sorts of persecution could not suppress their fanatical ardour. By 1881 their main objective was achieved: Czar Alexander II fell a victim to a terrorist conspiracy. This was, however, a Pyrrhic victory of the revolutionaries. Most of the members of the Central Committee were executed, while others were slowly dying in Siberian mines. After its supreme efforts, 'The Party of the Popular Will' was physically destroyed, and the new ruler, Alexander III, instead of compromise, initiated in 1881 a new policy of repression and reaction. This, however, did not stop the spread of socialist ideas in Russia. In the eighties, just as in the seventies, Marxists and Populists still formed the most influential group of Russian intelligentsia, and the whole intellectual and artistic life of the country was permeated by the spirit of political opposition and radical aspiration.

11. POPULISTS
AND THE WRITERS OF THE SOIL

IN the sixties and seventies, with vast numbers of new readers, with the commercialization of the book trade, with the demands of rising classes, with the expansion of education, the influence of literature was at its height. When Chernyshevsky wrote that 'Literature in Russia constitutes almost the sum total of its intellectual life,' he simply stated a fact. In a country deprived of the various outlets familiar to the West, a literary work was always a social event. Its moral and emotional impact was greater and broader than anywhere else in Europe. The writer was a teacher and a guide, and his activities were considered as the fulfilment of a lofty duty. Besides, the sixties were continuing the traditions of the Golden Age, and, in amount and quality, works published during this decade are truly impressive. It was precisely between 1860 and 1870 that the following novels, for instance, appeared in Russia: *Rudin, A Nest of Gentlefolk, On the Eve, Fathers and Sons,* and *Smoke,* by Turgenev; *The Humiliated and the Wronged, The Gambler, Crime and Punishment,* and *The Idiot,* by Dostoevsky; *The Cossacks* and *War and Peace,* by Tolstoy; *Oblomov* and *The Precipice,* by Goncharov; and there were many novels by Pisemsky, Leskov, Saltykov, and others. As a rule, prose prevailed in this period over poetry, and the spirit of realism triumphed; but there were many different kinds of realistic writing, and the literary scene presented great variety.

Together with the *rasnochintsy* came a grop of uncouth novelists who reported the facts of their own experience and depicted in a crude fashion the dark corners of Russian life. For instance, there were Nicholas Pomialovsky, son of a poor deacon who exposed the gruesome life in a provincial theological seminar where he had been flogged not less than 400 times (*Bursary School Sketches*), and Fedor Rechetnikov, son of a priest, who, in *The People of Podlipnoye,* gave an appalling picture of the life of poor folk in the north of Russia; and other writers followed suit with crude, down-to-earth descriptions of Russian *mores*. This school of factual writing was later hailed as the precursor of proletarian literature, and communist critics excused its sloppiness and artistic poverty as 'a reaction against the patrician gentility of the upper classes.'

While populist moods and ideas appeared in the works of Tolstoy, who created his own kind of populism, and Dostoevsky, whose popular tendencies were strongly tainted with religious slavophilism, a host of minor writers chose to represent either the new spirit of the intelligentsia, or the farmers and the common folk. The highly popular novels of the period were those by Alexander Sheller-Mikhailov, Gregory Machtet, Innokenty Omulevsky, or the navy sketches by Konstantin Staniukovich, all of them 'socially conscious,' all of them trying to reflect their times in a straight representational manner. These writers certainly succeeded in historically documenting an epoch; but as artists they occupy a very minor place. More successful from a purely literary standpoint were the numerous chroniclers of the village, like the moralistic and sentimental Nicholas Zlatovratsky, whose *The Foundations* depicted the class divisions within a rural commune, or the more critical Alexander Ertel, whose longwinded panorama of country life, *The Gardenins,* shows a remarkable sense of language.

Interesting as forerunners of Chekhov and Gorky are the writers of sketches, the ironical tramp Alexander Levitov, and the humorous Vassily Sleptzov. Most of these writers were connected with populism, not only ideologically but as active members of underground groups. Their defects and virtues all combined in Gleb Uspensky (1843-1902), the most important author of the whole movement. Like all his colleagues, he focussed his attention on 'the humiliated and the wronged,' on their poverty, drunkenness, and brutality. This son of a petty official was extremely susceptible to 'the travail and diseases of the conscience,' as Mikhailovsky, the leader of populism in the eighties, has put it. Like the 'repentant nobleman,' he took social injustice, poverty, or administrative abuse as a personal affront and he had a morbid sensitivity. His sketches of peasant life were highly popular. They represented facts on an almost ethnographic level, but Uspensky always related them to the larger political and social issues. He also corrected the current idealization of the peasant and did not hide the low level of peasant development. Uspensky's attitude marked a passage from idealistic to critical populism. The literary value of his works is very questionable: they resemble an enormous scrapbook, filled with sketches and reportage. Everything is tentative and rough, and his fiction is part sociological essay, part newspaper article. This kind of writing, however, created a precedent in Russia, and although it declined in the early twentieth century, it was resuscitated under communism.

Uspensky's personal drama contributed to his popularity: he reacted so deeply and violently to human sufferings and to the ills of his society that he went out of his mind and spent the last years of his life in an institution.

The wounded conscience of the intellectual disturbed by the unhappiness of the masses found its full expression in Nicholas Nekrassov (1821-77), a poet who became the idol of readers in the sixties and the seventies and whose role in Russian poetry goes far beyond his popularity. Son of a nobleman, he left his provincial estate and went to St. Petersburg in the forties to become a man of letters in search of literary fame. Before reaching his goal, he led the life of a tramp, starved, struggled for existence in the slums of the capital, and in general passed through all sorts of sordid experience. He worked as a literary hack, learned his idealism in Belinsky's circle, and his practical wisdom among crooks and ruthless moneymakers. Finally, he became a successful business man and made and spent a great deal of money. He was aggressive, clever, almost rapacious, and, as the editor of influential monthlies and the friend and publisher of great writers, played an enormous role in Russia's literary life. Most important, however, were his poems. In his early pieces he portrayed peasant types and Russian landscapes (the epic *Jack Frost; Orina, Soldier's Mother,* etc.), in a realistic and colloquial vein. His later poems expressed the grief and misery of millions of his countrymen, and their melancholy, almost despondent mood struck contemporaries as truly representative. Most of his larger poems, such as the popular *Who Finds Life Good in Russia?* or *Russian Women* (about Decembrists' wives who followed their husbands to the Siberian exile), as well as a number of minor stanzas, are topical and representational, mostly written in a vernacular idiom. On the other side, his lyrical confessions reflect the mood of the repentant nobleman who felt an idealistic love for the down-trodden and dreamed of heroic sacrifice in the fight for justice. Nekrassov believed in the social mission of poetry and stated: 'You may not be a poet but you must be a citizen.' His was the message of a radical intellectual with strong socialist inclinations, and it went to the heart of his contemporaries. Unlike many of the poets of his time who looked for inspiration to Greece or the Renaissance, like Shcherbina and Maikov, Nekrassov was an eminently national poet. His comments on current events spoke clearly to those who, like him, had faith in 'wretched and abundant, oppressed and powerful, weak and mighty Mother Russia.' As a man and as a poet, he was torn by the conflict between his revolutionary, altruistic ideals and his way of life. Young students who went into prison and exile repeating Nekrassov's stanza 'fate demands expiatory victims, the cause of freedom can be strong only if cemented by blood, nothing is free of cost,' did not suspect that their beloved bard led a highly opportunistic and often epicurean existence. This duality was the source of Nekrassov's genuine repentance and sufferings. He talked about them in sorrowful stanzas, and some of them acquired tragic accents, like that in which be owned his faults and begged pardon of his country: 'O Fatherland, forgive me all for the drop of blood I had in common with my people.'

Nekrassov's social poetry, as well as his poems of self-recrimination, continued the moral trend so typical of Russian literature. But while a Romantic like Lermontov was concerned with the individual in a world of isolation, pride, and evil, Nekrassov questioned man's behaviour in man's society and explored the twists of conscience resulting from social environment or political responsibility. The material and the language of his poetry were also highly challenging. He dealt with contemporary material, talked of railroads, banks, manual labour, prison camps, and Volga boatmen; and the obvious social purpose of this tendentious poetry was matched by its verbal boldness. Nekrassov drew on popular tradition and used all the devices of folklore. When his patrician critics complained that his poems 'smelled of muzhik,' they were absolutely right. Nekrassov introduced peasant modes and rhythms into written poetry, and worked deliberately at a 'depoetization of language.' His use of understatement and realistic detail were weapons in his struggle against Romantic convention. He reformed the poetry of his time as Gogol was supposed to have reformed the prose, but his actual value transcends historical bounds. It is not as the promoter of civic poetry that Nekrassov ranks with Russia's greatest poets. In the nineties, the symbolists were the first to emphasize the originality of his work, the sweep of his oratorical passages, the andante lacrimoso of his songs. 'He wept more effectively and beautifully than any other Russian poet,' remarked Chukovsky, and his slow, mournful lines, with their dactylic endings and prolonged vowels, sound like a solo in a choral group. His poetry has the genuine ring of popular music, of couplets recited at village reunions, of the lento of work-chants, of the sentimental ballads sung by peasant girls.

If Nekrassov was the poet of the radical intelligentsia, Saltykov-Shchedrin was its great satirist. Critical realism assumed in the works of this Russian Swift a violently negative character.

Mikhail Saltykov (1826-89), who wrote under the pen name of Shchedrin, was born into a family of ancient nobility, was educated at Pushkin's alma mater, the Lyceum of Tsarskoye Syelo, and as a civil servant rose to the rank of Deputy Governor of the Riazan and Tver provinces. When he resigned in 1862 he was already known as the author of sharp realistic sketches, but now he devoted himself exclusively to writing and to journalism. He shared with Nekrassov the editorship of radical monthlies and was considered by the intelligentsia as one of the foremost representatives of the anti-Czarist opposition. In his satirical writing he violently attacked all the abuses on the part of stupid administrators, the corruption of lazy bureaucrats, the ignorance of the ruling classes, the backwardness of aristocratic reactionaries, and finally the greed and obscurantism of the new rising capitalists. In his highly popular and symbolic story of an imaginary town he presented the whole history of Czarist Russia as a long series of barbarisms and mistakes, ridiculed emperors and ministers, and laughed at the reactionary measures by which autocracy attempted to stop the expansion of progressive ideas. Written in an Aesopic language which protected them from the censor's blue pencil, Saltykov's allegories and allusions were, however, clear to his readers. Some of his 'mots' were current all over Russia and found their way permanently into the language. Even though most of his satires are topical and refer to events and conditions at a given period, one can still feel their biting vigour. What made Saltykov different from other satirists (it is interesting to compare his *History of a Town* with Anatole France's *L'Ile des Penguins,* for example) is the intensity of his indignation. Like a Juvenal, he lashed his enemies with a stinging whip, and his mordant wit and spiteful irony have a force and a fire we can feel even now. The most lasting of Saltykov's novels is, however, *The Golovlyovs,* a gloomy, almost tragic description of a landowner's family presided over by a despotic and greedy mother and ruined by a hypocritical and rapacious son, Little Judas, whose name became the symbol of avaricious pettiness and deceit among Russian intellectuals. The cruel realism of this *exposé* recurs, although in a mitigated form, in *The Old Times of Pochekhonye,* a penetrating study of serfdom and the Russian way of life in the pre-reform era. These two works, as well as the amusing political *Fairy Tales,* are amongst the most significant expressions of critical realism. After 1930 communist critics in the U.S.S.R. tried to build up Saltykov as a genuine 'revolutionary democrat,' playing down his populist sympathies and connexions.

The opposition to revolutionary tendencies and to populism, without ever reaching the proportions of the liberal movement, was, however, very strong in the seventies and the eighties. Two theorists of absolutism led the right wing. Konstantin Leontiev (1831-91), a remarkably talented religious thinker, novelist and essayist, a great believer in Russia's imperial mission in the Orient, and a supporter of intransigent and punitive autocracy; and Nicholas Danilevsky (1822-95), a naturalist and a Slavophile historian, an anti-liberal and anti-capitalist who insisted on the immutability of Russia's political regime and introduced the notion of national 'cultural types,' later taken up by the German Oswald Spengler. In fiction the conservative school was very active already in the sixties when Pisemsky in his *Stormy Sea* represented the 'nihilists' as villains and embezzlers, and Leskov, in his *No Way Out* denounced the 'liberal drums' and the 'bearded and bespectacled babblers.' Later the same Leskov hit at the revolutionaries in his *At Daggers Drawn,* a melodramatic *exposé* of crimes and treachery, akin to the anti-revolutionary 'thrillers' by Vsevolod Krestovsky and Victor Kliushnikov. Dostoevsky's *The Possessed* partly belongs in the same category.

Disagreement with the radical movement and reaction against the 'invasion of the *rasnochintsy*' were also voiced by various groups of patrician writers who attempted to bring literature closer to the idealism of the forties. Pavel Annenkov (1812-87), an excellent memoirist and friend of Turgenev, and Apollon Grigoriev, a Romantic poet whose gypsy ballads and St. Petersburg poems have a great charm and whose articles against the positivists combined Schelling's philosophy with Slavophilism in a new guise, both wrote in the name of pure art against Chernyshevsky and his disciples. Various patrician poets formed an important group and defended the principles of 'pure art.' The most important among them were Apollon Maikov, an admirer of the Greeks and a faithful Christian (1821-97), and Count Alexis Tolstoy (1817-75), author of the highly popular poetic trilogy, *The Death of Ivan the Terrible, Czar Fedor* and *Czar Boris,* and of lyrical pieces of great delicacy. Although a conservative, Tolstoy made fun of bureaucracy and belonged to a group of poets who, under the fictitious identity of Kuzma Prutkov, created hilarious lampoons and puns directed against the narrowness of the bureaucrats. Other minor poets, such as the gloomy Konstantin Sluchevsky (1837-1904), or the epicurean Alexis Apukhtin (1841-93), or the more liberal Polonsky and Plescheyev, were mostly read in the eighties and the nineties, as was Athanassy Shenshin-Fet, a pantheistic poet strongly influenced by Schopenhauer, whose works he translated into Russian. Fet's poems on love and nature were not appreciated until the end of the century, however; and in the sixties his lines on 'whispers, shy breath, nightingale's trills' were quoted as examples of 'brainless aestheticism.' Stern radicals and socialists missed his elusive music and ignored his delicacy of touch and the rhythmical virtuosity of his poems, which caught the connecting link between 'the dark delirium of the soul and the vague scent of herbs.' Fet's exaltation of the 'fleeting dreams' of life coloured by pleasure found, however, a response among the decadents and the symbolists, who glorified Fet as a master of melodiousness, as a 'mystical aesthete,' and as a poet of the first magnitude.

One place apart was occupied by a poet whose stature surpassed the limitations of groups or schools, Fedor Tiutchev (1803-73). Son of a rich landowner, he became a career diplomat, spent twenty-two years abroad in Russian embassies, then occupied high posts in the Foreign Office. His work attracted no attention until 1854 and was not appreciated until a great deal later. The poems he wrote in moments of leisure (only about 400 in all, including translations) are remarkable for their unity, compactness, and elegance. Couched in a highly literary and somewhat archaic style which links them to the eighteenth century rather than to Pushkin, these fragmentary, philosophical, almost aphoristic verses present reflections on the primeval Chaos, the source of all things, and nature, 'this golden pall thrown over a nameless precipice.' For Tiutchev, life 'is surrounded by dreams, even as the earth by the ocean, and the waves of the elements beat noisily upon the shore.' The eternal pair, Death and Sleep, as well as the passions, are part of Chaos. Chaos, or Night, occupies the soul together with the light of Day, and this breeds discord. Man's duality has, however, other causes: he does not want to submit to the universal order, and his reason rebels against the world. 'The thinking reed does not join in the chorus of waves, in the harmonious melody of the universe; he is the only one to murmur in protest and to sing his own song.' Leo Tolstoy could not listen without tears to Tiutchev's pantheistic lines: 'all things are within me, I am in all things, let me partake of annihilation, let me be diffused in the slumbering Universe; nothing leaves any trace, and it is so easy not to be.' Along with poems which embodied this 'cosmic consciousness,' Tiutchev wrote poignant lyrics of love in which passion and melancholy are intermingled. Although Tiutchev expressed in his poems the aspirations of the Russian religious mind and anticipated the symbolists, he also wrote topical verse which, together with his pamphlets in French, reveal a curious mixture of conservatism and Slavophile messianism.

In any case, his anti-liberal contemporaries believed that the oratorical declamatory swing and the old-fashioned gait of his poetry made Tiutchev their ally and hailed him as a 'pure Russian.' They applied this label to a whole group of prose writers who could be classified with more validity as 'writers of the soil.' These writers had in common a preference for representing national types and environment, paying a great deal of attention to Russian customs and traditions, depicting lower and middle classes rather than the nobility or the intellectuals, and usually writing in that idiomatic, almost vernacular manner which denied the genteel aristocratic tradition of Karamzin and Turgenev. Despite diversity of temperament and political opinion, the writers of the soil longed for the 'resumption of the lost unity between educated society and the large popular masses,' and some of them were plainly akin to the populists. Some critics, stressing the strong national flavour of Ostrovsky's plays, include him in this group, but others argue that he was highly critical of the environment he depicted, while true writers of the soil were sympathetic to the 'old Russian' way of life. Serghei Aksakov (1791-1859), one of the most remarkable Russian 'ocular realists' and the author of beautiful idyllic recollections (*Family Chronicles, The Childhood of Bagrov's Grandson*), can also be included (with some reservations) in the category of patrician writers who were close to Mother Earth. Less doubtful is the case of Alexis Pisemsky (1820-81), a vigorous novelist and a staunch follower of the realistic trend, who added a few examples to the gallery of superfluous noblemen. Pisemsky, himself an impoverished nobleman and a civil servant who lived many years in the provinces, knew best the peasants and the small burghers, and he caught them in racy and shrewd works, some of which, such as the classic *A Thousand Souls* (1858), or the remarkable tragic play, *A Hard Lot* (1869), placed him immediately after the great masters of realism. 'He smells of the wildwood, of the black loam, of what the French call the *parfum de terroir*,' declared Annenkov in his essay on this anti-European who never missed an opportunity to express his dislike of foreigners and of Western customs.

In many instances the writers of the soil developed the kind of regional distinctness which was bound to emerge in such a vast and multi-national continent as Russia. One of the pioneers was Pavel Melnikov (1819-93), who wrote under the pen name of Andrei Pechersky. His epic novels *In the Woods* and *On the Hills* were devoted to the life and habits of the Old Believers (or Old Ritualists), who fled from the persecutions of the Church and of the government and established prosperous colonies in the Urals and in Siberia, where they were able to maintain their ancient traditions intact. A large number of Sectarians, and the richest merchant families in Moscow and on the Volga in the nineteenth century, came from Old Believers stock. Melnikov's novels revealed the whole world of their peculiar customs and passionate personalities and reproduced their seventeenth-century speech. (The linguistic and ethnographic value of Melnikov's work was highly praised by Gorky and other twentieth-century writers.) A lesser regionalist was Dimitri Mamin (1852-1912), called Sibiriak (The Siberian). His naturalistic descriptions of the bourgeoisie of the Urals and Asiatic Russia were formless and lacked artistry, but they had a certain illustrative vigour.

But Nicholas Leskov (1831-95) was by far the greatest writer of the soil. His first novels, *No Way Out* (1864) and *At Daggers Drawn* (1871), sharply denouncing the radical youth, made him taboo in liberal circles, which in the seventies meant the majority of educated society. Leskov was persecuted as a reactionary; but during the last twenty years of his life he was also labelled 'subversive' by the defenders of autocracy. Only after his death did the work of this original and independent writer receive full appreciation beyond changing political moods.

The range of his work was vast. He depicted small clergy in his remarkable novel *Cathedral Folk,* with its memorable priest Tuberosov, who fights against the Church bureaucrats, and the athletic deacon Achilla, who uses his fists for 'kindly Christian persuasion'; and his novels *The Circumvented* and *The Islanders,* reveal the 'nihilists,' the *rasnochintsy,* and the bohemians of St. Petersburg. His *Old Days of Plodomasovo* and *A Family in Decline* are excellent historical chronicles of provincial nobility; and his numerous short stories and novelettes—perhaps his highest achievements—present a motley procession of artisans, tradesmen, adventurers, peasants, officials, middle-class ladies and merchant girls. The picaresque *Enchanted Wanderer* or the stylized *The Sealed Angel,* as well as the *Tale of the Squint-Eyed Left-Handed Smith from Tula and the Steel Flea* have a strong flavour of Russian folklore. They all evince Leskov's ver-

bal virtuosity, his humour, his Gogolian bent for linguistic
grotesquerie, his delight in twisting and playing on words,
his feeling for the various levels of popular speech, and
his love for slang, puns, jingles, and amusing folk expressions.

In fact, Leskov's language is so colourful and hilarious, his style so brilliantly amusing, his stories so packed
with incidents and funny turns, that many readers and
critics saw only his entertainment value and disregarded
Leskov's profound religious feeling, his interest in the
hidden roots of national character and his predilection
for 'righteous men,' manifestations of a Slavic Don
Quixote. Many of his characters pass through the purga-
tory of crime and lust; but his sinners always look for
salvation in repentance and good deeds. Leskov is one of
the few Russian writers of the nineteenth century who
deliberately set out to present positive characters. There
in such a love of man and of his goodness and such a
faith in the basic health and vigour of the Russian national tradition, which he explored in so many different
ways, that the totality of his witty, rich, and often contradictory work, presents a more complete and more
genuine picture of nineteenth-century Russia than the
most famous writings of more popular authors. Although
Chekhov, first of all, saw Leskov's contrasts and defined
him as a combination of 'a graceful Frenchman with an
unfrocked priest,' it was Gorky who underlined his national significance: 'he did not write about the muzhik,
the Nihilist, the landowner—he wrote about the Russian.
One feels that in each of his tales, Leskov was mainly
preoccupied with the destiny of the whole of Russia rather
than with that of any individual. He is one of the foremost Russian writers, and his work took in all of Russia.'

12. DOSTOEVSKY

DOSTOEVSKY'S first novel, *Poor Folk,* was published in
1846, and his last, *The Brothers Karamazov,* in 1880.
In the span of these thirty-five years he wrote a series of
works the impact of which on the Western world has
been more shattering and lasting than that of any other
Russian writer, except Tolstoy. While critics and psychol-

ogists try to explain Dostoevsky's power analytically and argue about his insanity or his morbidity, millions of men and women everywhere continue to enjoy the stirring and frightening experience that is the reading of his books.

Fedor Dostoevsky was born in 1821 in Moscow, where his father, an impoverished nobleman, held the post of resident physician at a charity hospital. The family had small living quarters in the hospital grounds, and the child, at an early age, became familiar with suffering, misfortune, and death. He was brought up in an atmosphere of strict discipline and religious piety under his morose and authoritarian father. His mother was kind and sickly; she died when he was sixteen. Sent afterwards to the St. Petersburg School of Military Engineers, he spent there four depressing unhappy years. His father had been murdered by his mishandled serfs; Fedor remained alone, without money or friends. He detested his school and had but one passion: literature. Shortly after graduation he resigned his position as a military draughtsman and devoted himself to writing. After years of poverty and privation, he published his first novel, *Poor Folk,* which met with a certain success. He published other novelettes and tales and wrote feverishly, brimming with projects and ideas. Then a catastrophe befell him: he was arrested as a member of a clandestine group of young idealists who discussed Utopian socialism and dreamed of freedom. In 1849 Dostoevsky, together with his friends, was sentenced to death and brought to the execution place in a public square before the firing squad. At the very last moment an official came forward and announced the Czar's clemency, and the death sentence was commuted into one of penal servitude. Before Dostoevsky could recover his senses, he found himself in irons and on his way to Siberia.

After this monstrous experience of sham execution, he spent four years as a convict at hard labour, surrounded by murderers and other criminals, and had to submit to treatment so inhuman that only glimpses of it can be caught in his later work, especially in *Memoirs from the House of the Dead.* In 1854 he was sent as a private to an infantry regiment in Semipalatinsk, an Asiatic hellhole. In 1857 he married a young consumptive widow. He was thirty-eight years old when in 1858, after nine years of all kinds of ordeals, he was finally allowed to return to St.

Petersburg and to resume his place in literature. From 1859 and until his death in 1881 he was incessantly active as a novelist, journalist, and editor. His first wife died in 1864 and two years later he married his stenographer; despite the difference of age (she was twenty and he was forty-four) she became a loving and understanding companion. In the sixties and seventies Dostoevsky published his most important works: *The Humiliated and Wronged* (1861), *Notes from the Underground* (1864), *Crime and Punishment* (1866), *The Idiot* (1868), *The Possessed* (1871), *A Raw Youth* (1875), *The Diary of a Writer* (1876-80), and *The Brothers Karamazov* (1880). All these works brought him fame, yet this did not make things easier for him. He had to write hurriedly in order to fight off poverty, and he was in precarious health and subject, after his imprisonment, to frequent and exhausting fits of epilepsy. During his travels abroad his passion for gambling led to disaster. There were further conflicts with the censors and the government, there were quarrels and feuds with his colleagues and former friends, but over and above all this, there were his ecstatic flights, his carnal temptations, and the rambling of his tormented soul in search of God, harmony, and truth.

Dostoevsky's literary roots are all too clear. He started in the wake of the Russian Realistic school, and imitated Gogol in his first novels and stories, especially in *Poor Folk* and *The Double*. But he was also strongly influenced by European Romantics; E. T. A. Hoffman's images of split personality and of the fantastic power of evil, Victor Hugo's humanitarianism, and the rapid pace of adventure novels by minor French authors such as Eugène Sue, greatly appealed to him. These trends converge in his novels, which are constructed like thrillers and unroll a stream of most unusual events, being filled at the same time with accurate detail and description.

Dostoevsky started by following the great Russian tradition of compassion for the little man. In *Poor Folk,* Makar Devushkin, a humble clerk who has not enough money to rent a room all for himself, falls in love with a poor young girl but is unable to save her from marrying her former seducer, a wealthy landowner. Both their lives are ruined, and nothing can be done about it. In *The Double,* a novel which offers very important clues for understanding Dostoevsky, another governmental clerk, Golyadkin, becomes a complete schizophrenic. In order to escape the narrow pattern of a miserable existence, he creates the image of his own aggressive and successful self, a double, and his dream materializes and acquires independent life, until Golyadkin is taken to a lunatic asylum. The theme of split personality and of the double which lurks in every man is combined here with a study in depth of inferiority complex and of pathological and erotic drives.

These two works, as well as all others stories of this first period, bear but a superficial resemblance to Gogol's *The Overcoat* and *The Diary of a Madman*. In fact, for Dostoevsky the underdog's unhappy fate in a hostile universe is not a simple matter for pity; his victims of environment raise directly or indirectly the problem of man's condition on earth. The order of things is questioned not only from the social and moral but also from the metaphysical point of view. Besides, Gogolian caricatures and grotesques are replaced by complex characters who reveal a great deal of morbidity.

In the second period of Dostoevsky's development (between 1854 and 1864), there is, however, a shift of emphasis, and the 'defeated ones' are no longer resigned to their status—instead, they become more conscious of human and divine injustice and they claim their rights. The plea for the little man is resumed in *The Humiliated and Wronged*. Fifteen years after his first novel, under cover of a story which contains all the paraphernalia of a cheap mystery thriller (rape, murder, a lost will, illegitimate children, false identity, ruthless villains, sentimental love), Dostoevsky expanded on his main theme. He combined the psychological, the symbolic, and the philosophical elements in his narrative, stressed the clash of man's contradictory drives, and sharpened the conflict between two types of humanity: the weak, submissive ones who have masochistic inclinations, confronted (and exploited or martyred) by ruthless 'masters of life' who, with sadistic relish, reject moral codes and transgress the boundaries of good and evil. The virus of transgression, however, infects their victims, who finally refuse to accept their place in the cellar of the social edifice. Those 'men from the underground' either protest intellectually or resort to the miracle of chance, like the hero of *The*

Gambler who believes he can 'correct' the injustice of his social position by a lucky win at roulette. The hero of *Notes from the Underground,* one of Dostoevsky's most significant works, rationalizes his passivity and his sado-masochistic tendencies. He claims that action is typical of stupid, simple men while intelligence leads to doubt and inertia. Betterment of society is impossible because of the irrationality and the contradictions in human nature; the trouble therefore lies not in man's condition but in his mind and body, since he is basically rebellious, cruel, unreasonable, and prefers danger to safety and chance to order.

In the third and final stage of Dostoevsky's literary and ideological evolution, the man from the underground comes to the surface and, in the person of Raskolnikov (*Crime and Punishment*), chooses open rebellion as the only means of changing his destiny.[1] Raskolnikov also has a theory: he divides mankind into two main groups—the trembling multitude of common men and the daring minority of exceptional individuals who have the right to transgress the conventional rules of social law and custom. In order to prove to himself that he belongs to the second category, Raskolnikov kills an old hag of a moneylender and her simple-hearted sister. In the ensuing conflict between his rational self and his emotional sensitivity, he comes to the conclusion, however, that his intellectual crime does not constitute a valid proof. Incapable of placing himself beyond good and evil and of solving the problem of free will by sheer self-assertion, Raskolnikov learns his lesson the hard way. Through suffering and nightmares he arrives at the realization of his error—that human behaviour cannot be prescribed by rational calculation, that the emotional, irrational side of man's nature is far more important, that each person has his own intrinsic value however sinful or useless or obnoxious he may appear to be. Raskolnikov then recognizes the eternal truth of Christian morality as revealed to him by Sonia, a prostitute and a social pariah.

---

[1] While several critics have stressed the analogy between Raskolnikov and Rastignac in Balzac's *Père Goriot*, less attention has been paid to the link between Dostoevsky's rebels and Lermontov's *A Hero of Our Own Times*; Pechorin is undoubtedly one of the first 'supermen' in Russian literature. Another interesting comparison could be made between *The Gambler* and Herman from Pushkin's *Queen of Spades*.

The main themes of *Crime and Punishment*—freedom and power, the limits of accepted morals, the opposition between the herd and the leaders, the man and the superman were later taken up by Nietzsche who recognized Dostoevsky as one of his masters. But the author of *So Spake Zarathustra* and *Beyond Good and Evil* could certainly not agree with the ending of this novel in which, for the first time in Dostoevsky's work, the problem of redemption and purification through suffering was put forward in terms of religious faith, and more precisely, Christian dogma.

It is usually accepted that from 1865, when *Crime and Punishment* was written, until his death, Dostoevsky was chiefly concerned with religion and Christianity. Although the words of one of his characters, 'God tormented me all my life,' could certainly be applied to him, Dostoevsky was more prone to ask questions and argue about problems than to offer solutions and to affirm positive belief. He transferred into his novels the debate which went on incessantly in his mind and heart, and through his heroes he always argued with himself. Already in *The Idiot,* written after *Crime and Punishment,* one is struck by the ambiguity of the main hero, Prince Myshkin, a Christ-like figure who possesses all the virtues of tolerance, goodness, and sincerity, who believes that the law of love is more efficient than the law of strength, but who fails to avoid disaster around him. His passive Christianity is unable to cope with the ills and passions of society, and he collapses under the double burden of insanity and murder.

It is quite clear that Dostoevsky's preoccupation with crime was not merely that of a novelist who discovers in it a technical device for building suspense. Transgression, seen as one of man's most natural and fateful actions, was his focal point in the discussion of the limits of freedom and basic human nature. According to his pessimistic view, man was irresistibly attracted by evil, but his duality made him oscillate between the pleasure of inflicting pain and challenging God, and the desire to submit to the Law and to accept suffering for the glory of God. In general, Dostoevsky presented all his characters in the flux and struggle of their inner conflicts, in the dynamism of their contradictions, in the dialectical development of their opposites. These psychological contradictions were usually projected in his novels against a topical picture of Russian society. While Raskolnikov in *Crime and Punishment* could be interpreted as a typical nihilist of the sixties, the revolutionary movement of the seventies was hit by Dostoevsky in his novel-parody, novel-pamphlet, *The Possessed,* in which he gave free rein to his angry feelings against liberalism, socialism, and radicalism, those very idols he revered in his youth, and revealed all his biting sarcasm and irony and humour. Conceived as a rebuff and an *exposé* of revolutionaries, *The Possessed,* however, went beyond the boundaries of polemic and brought out with customary Dostoevskian intensity, his main anxieties and the problems of faith, atheism, and will-to-power. Piotr Verkhovensky, a demonic revolutionary, is one of the main characters in this extraordinary novel where fantasy and realism coexist in perilous equilibrium. He uses knaves, fools, and cowards for his conspiratorial purposes, and dreams of a godless society with enforced equality; but in the meantime he accepts every means to achieve his end and applies to everybody the Jesuitical principle: 'violence for the body, and deceit for the soul.' He has difficulty, however, with Stavroghin, the man he hopes to promote as sham leader of an uprising. This 'dark hero' is perfectly capable of crime and sacrifice and is attracted by light and darkness alike. He is the symbol of an unchannelled force, of undirected and self-destroying energy. Both men are possessed by demons, but Stavroghin does not yield to Verkhovensky. He accepts defeat and prefers suicide to a futile life of deception. His death in the fourteenth in a narrative that seems highly melodramatic even to habitual readers of Dostoevsky. Of extreme importance to the understanding of Dostoevsky are the minor characters in the novel: Kirillov, with his dream of men who would overcome fear of death and become Gods, who opposes his formula to Christianity and commits suicide in order to assert his freedom and will power; Shatov, who ends by believing in Russia's high mission; and Shigalev, who pictures the socialist state as a totalitarian dictatorship.

All the main themes of Dostoevsky found their fullest expression in *The Brothers Karamazov,* a novel which can be interpreted on many levels and which has many symbolic intimations and hidden meanings. It is probably Dostoevsky's 'Divina Commedia,' his highest achievement both in psychological insight, variety of character, and intellectual richness. Here again, the plot revolves around a crime and its detection. Two legitimate sons of the old sinner Karamazov, the intellectual Ivan and the impulsive Dimitri, have personal reasons for wishing the death of their lustful and cynical father who is finally murdered. Although all the circumstantial evidence points at Dimitri, and although Ivan considers himself the theoretical instigator of the parricide, the actual slayer is Smerdyakov, a bastard born out of Karamazov's sordid affair with a demented tramp. The fourth son, Alesha, fresh from a monastery, desperately tries to pacify his brothers and to calm the raging passions around him. He cannot, however, prevent Dimitri's condemnation by a peasant jury, Ivan's brain fever, and Smerdyakov's suicide.

As a central figure in the novel, Ivan is akin to Raskolnikov. He is also a rebel, but his rebellion is more abstract, and more sustained philosophically. He is a dialectician who is weighing the arguments of faith and disbelief. If there is no God and no immortality for the soul, then virtue is man's invention, and everything is permissible. In his metaphysical analysis Ivan comes to the conclusion that no promise of universal harmony can follow from man's sufferings and plight; and he is ready to give back his 'life ticket' if God has based the order of things on children's tears, on torture, death, and injustice. Those are too high a price for any heavenly compensation. In the name of humanity's dignity and happiness, Ivan renounces the cruel Lord and dreams of a society where men might be virtuous for their own sake, without fear of hell or expectation of divine reward. But like Raskolnikov, Ivan collapses in the isolation of his intellectual search, which ignores love and nature and which ends in an ethical 'no man's land' where freedom is sterile and useless.

His brother Dimitri is at the opposite pole: his emotional moods change constantly, and he believes that all the sources of evil lie in the human heart. God and the Devil fight there without respite, man is alternately attracted by the vision of Beauty, by the Madonna, and by the lure of the cities of the plain, by Sodom and Gomorrha. This is his curse, to be contradictory, to contain both virtue and vice in equal proportions.

The Grand Inquisitor, in a fantastic story which Ivan

tells his brother Alesha, is also of the opinion that human defects are the main obstacle on the road to God and salvation. In fact, he is convinced that happiness excludes freedom, that Christ's main error was to offer freedom of choice in knowledge of good and evil to the average man, for only extraordinary, exceptional individuals can sustain the burden of liberty. Thus Christianity, which demands a free act of faith, is impossible on earth, is unbearable for the common man. When Christ returns among men, the Grand Inquisitor puts Him in prison and reproaches Him for having set impossibly high standards and for having ignored material needs. 'Not by bread alone,' but how can one live without bread? Christianity has failed to create a society, and now the Grand Inquisitor and his friends are going to repair Christ's mistakes and 'correct' His work. Men prefer security to freedom, satiety to dreams, and they are perfectly satisfied when ruled by authority (for the will), miracle (for the imagination), and mystery (for the reason). They are safely led into an artificial paradise, a well-planned, comfortable existence where they are even allowed to sin— and they obey totalitarian leaders who know how to satisfy the appetites of this rebellious contradictory childish animal.

This distortion of Christianity, in terms which curiously predict the basic arguments of fascism and communism, is refuted by Alesha. He is another Christlike figure. Mild and good, he rejects violence, deceit, and lust for power. But unlike the Idiot, he is not a simple embodiment of the Christian spirit—he is a Christian knight, actively struggling for his faith, trying to live in compliance with the precepts of love, brotherhood, and self-sacrifice, after Christ's example. His religion does not consist of dogma; it radiates warmth, compassion, and understanding, it promotes repentance and it strives for a living Christian society. Thus a promise of Resurrection brings hope to the tortured and twisted world of these restless heroes.

In the last years of his life Dostoevsky attempted to give this hope concrete meaning. An atheistic socialist in his youth, he underwent a political and religious crisis during his Siberian exile, and he returned to St. Petersburg a defender of autocracy and of the Church. Despite his conversion the very dynamism of his intellect and the

intensity of his emotions gave an extremist stamp to all
his writings. He was afraid of the provocative and anarchical impact of his novels and tried to discipline his own
nature, to penalize his rebellious spirit, and to genuflect
before the Czar and Greek Orthodox dogma and ritual.
This spiritual revolutionary who challenged accepted
ideas, whose art registered, like a seismograph, all the
eruptions of passion and all the convulsions of the unconscious, proclaimed his worship of thrones and altars
and his submission to established civic and clerical orders. No wonder that many Greek Orthodox dignitaries
and Czarist officials remained suspicious of so strange a
parishioner whose ardent breath had a smell of brimstone
about it.

Dostoevsky preached a general compliance to authority, justified coercive measures and reprisals against revolutionaries, sided with the most reactionary circles in
Russian society, and expressed his hope that a solid wall
of absolutism and religion would protect Russia against
revolution. From his apocalyptic visions of the future, he
predicted an approaching upheaval in Western Europe.
Strongly influenced by the Slavophiles, he believed that
Russian Christianity, in its love and mercy, was superior
to power-hungry Catholicism and to dry, rationalistic
Protestantism. Here again, his opinions reflected his
duality. In his letters from abroad and in various passages
in his novels, he drew angry pictures of the meanness of
petty-bourgeois France and of German smugness and
brutality; he was highly critical of England and often sar-
castic about Italy. Yet, at the same time, he loved Europe. Ivan Karamazov called it his 'most cherished cemetery' and promised to kiss its every tombstone. In his
famous speech on Pushkin (1880), which seemed to can-
cel the quarrel between Westernizers and Slavophiles,
Dostoevsky declared that Europe was a second fatherland
for the Russians and he called his countrymen true Eu-
ropeans. In the same speech he formulated his messianic
nationalism: Russia was destined to accomplish the union
of all nations in a common cause, in the free accord of all
peoples. Two traits of Russian character made him believe in this Utopia: the Russian national idea was universality ('to be Russian means to be universal') and
'Russian people, despite their bestiality, have Jesus Christ
in their heart.' This religious populism allotted the prin-

cipal role to the Greek Orthodox Church and envisioned a sort of theocratic millennium when State would become Church. Thus Russia would bring about universal peace and the reunion of all peoples as her contribution to the European community. This dream gives a special flavour to many of Dostoevsky's statements, in which he becomes not only a spokesman of nationalism but also a partisan of reaction and a spokesman for man's complete obedience, humility, and acquiescence. These sentiments, however, are to be found mostly in his articles and essays. In his novels artistic truth and the fervour of his spirit transforms even his worst political platitudes and social errors into a passionate plea for mankind.

Dostoevsky has discovered so much about our emotions and thoughts, has explored so deeply the human psyche, has made such astonishing revelations about our repressed drives and pathological complexes, that the modern world has hailed him as a master of the psychological novel. Some of his descriptions, for instance those of the epileptic fit, of fever, of anguish, of schizophrenia, of sadism, are so precise that they serve as illustrations in the study of clinical psychology. But Dostoevsky's psychological novel, often disguised as a mystery story, is actually a novel of ideas, and the latter are not merely discussed by various characters but incarnate in them to such an extent that problems and concepts never remain as abstractions: they are lived through in a highly personal and intense manner by passionate men and women who move on the Dostoevskian stage in despair, pain, lust, and madness. Everything acquires strange exaggerated proportions in these nightmare tales of almost unbearable suspense. Happenings race at a vertiginous speed, days and nights are packed with events (the action of *Crime and Punishment* takes place in nine days), intrigues and money litigations alternate with diabolical conspiracies, and fire, rape, murder, and suicide follow homicide, insanity, and blackmail. Starving students and saintly prostitutes, masochistic maidens and sadistic belles, gambling lovers and scheming adolescents, assassins and intellectuals, drunken buffoons and nihilists, monks and sinners, the pure-of-heart and philosophers, men from the underground and God-seekers—all these unforgettable characters pass in a fantastic cavalcade of passion and frenzy. These tragedies, filled with dialogues, monologues, and stage effects, reveal not only the tremendous imaginative power of their creator, but also all the pitfalls and aspirations of human nature which Dostoevsky was probing with a ruthlessness bordering on voluptuousness and with a sensitivity to pain akin to masochistic delight—but always with a clairvoyance of terrifying intensity, as if the eye were glimpsing heaven and hell through clouds riven by a thunderbolt. It is irrelevant whether the reader agrees with Dostoevsky's view of man, with his religion, or with his ideas. What makes Dostoevsky one of the most modern of writers is the fire of his exaltation and negation, the utter boldness with which he investigates the fundamentals of life and society.[1]

13. TOLSTOY

IT is common critical practice to make a precise differentiation between Dostoevsky and Tolstoy. Dostoevsky is usually called a subjective and Tolstoy an objective writer of epic magnitude. Merezhkovsky defines the first as 'the seer of the spirit' and the second as 'the seer of the flesh.' Other critics oppose Dostoevsky's irrationality and pessimism to Tolstoy's rational and optimistic view of man. Nothing is more superficial than such generalizations but they originate in the striking differences in the personality and the work of the two great novelists. While Dostoevsky expressed, in a truly Romantic vein, his ideas and anxieties through larger-than-life characters in situations of crisis, Tolstoy, a thorough realist and

[1] After his death, Dostoevsky's fame continued to grow in Russia and in the rest of the world. The Communist revolution, however, challenged his status. Even though a number of documents, essays, and treatises on his life and work were published in Soviet Russia in the early twenties (together with a good edition of his collected works in thirteen volumes), Dostoevsky was denounced by party officials and critics as the spokesman of reaction and an ideological enemy of the new regime. For more than twenty years, between 1932 and 1954, one could not write the whole truth about Dostoevsky in Russia, and some of his works such as Notes from the Underground, The Possessed, and The Brothers Karamazov, were not allowed to be reprinted. Only in 1956 was Dostoevsky officially 'rehabilitated' and a new edition of all his works made available to Soviet readers. Despite all these political vicissitudes, he remains one of the most influential and widely read Russian masters in all walks of Soviet society.

a staunch anti-Romantic, described himself and all the actualities of his life in their concrete, perceptible reality. Dostoevsky's work is utterly personal in so far as he endows the creatures of his imagination (who often do not resemble him) with all the flights and intricacies of his own mind. Tolstoy's work, even when he populates it with hundreds of life-size figures of unequalled variety, is definitely autobiographical. He is always in the centre of his universe. He started his literary career with reminiscences (*Childhood, Boyhood,* and *Youth,* 1852-56); and he did not bother to disguise himself in later works (*A Landowner's Morning, Family Happiness*). He is the Olenin of *The Cossacks,* the Levin of *Anna Karenina,* the Eugene of *The Devil,* and the Nekhludov of *Resurrection.* He filled his books with the reality of his struggles or with explanations of his intimate problems, and when he felt that fiction did not suit his purpose any longer, he forsook art for a more simple and direct medium, and wrote essays, letters, and argumentative essays. It was not enough for him to be a writer: he wanted to be, and became, a preacher, a philosopher, the founder of a new religion, a critic of society, and a fighter for the renovation of mankind—and his gigantic figure belongs not only to fiction—by the end of the nineteenth century it occupied the foreground of the spiritual stage of the world. His influence in all domains was so strong, his impact on Russian thought and life as a precursor of the revolution so profound, his moral leadership so universal that he appears as the greatest man ever produced in Russia.

Many critics and readers reproach Tolstoy with his inconsistency and his contradictions. Some glorify the writer but vilify the moralist, others are enthusiastic about his works but disappointed in his life, and a great majority cut Tolstoy in pieces and are afraid to face the totality of that strange and grandiose phenomenon that bears his name. The trouble probably arises from the fact that he had both an extraordinary lust of life and an equally strong religious curiosity. Nobody was as much a realist, and nobody enjoyed every manifestation of life, for sheer delight of being, as fully as this ascetic seeker after God bent on renunciation and sacrifice.

Tolstoy was a vigorous man whose senses were as sharp as his memory; he felt intensely and he could remember or imagine with precision sensations, emotions, and physical details. In a way he was like the Uncle Eroshka, the old hunter in *The Cossacks* who obeyed the call to life, was in perfect accord with nature and believed (Tolstoy often said so) that the only aim of life was life itself. Tolstoy, who loved human beings as well as animals, who wrote wonderfully about dogs and horses, who depicted the fall of an ash tree with the same feeling as the death of man, filled all his novels and stories with the very pulse of being, with the plenitude of existence. In this, he was expressing the vigour of his race, the basic pagan vitality of the Russians. Whoever makes quick generalizations about the gloomy and pessimistic aura which envelops Russian literature would be in great difficulty when confronted with the affirmative, optimistic, and positive work of Tolstoy.

Tolstoy's capacity for living and reliving every instant explains the spell and the form of his great novels. In *War and Peace,* for example, there is no carefully constructed plot. Instead, the action flows like a river, like time itself. Whatever happens to Prince André, to Pierre, to Natasha, or to their kin, is represented in the flux of development. It has been often stated that not unlike the works of the Great Victorians, particularly of Trollope and George Eliot, who probably had influenced him, Tolstoy's epics—*War and Peace* and *Anna Karenina*—are family novels. But they are very peculiar specimens of the genre. Events in them are completely subordinated to the notion of time; space, as a *leit-motiv,* plays an important role, as E. M. Forster remarked; they have no beginning or end; and they avoid the devices of suspense or dramatic climax, of which Dostoevsky made such large use. Each episode stands out in its own right, complete in itself. No climaxes highlight the unrolling of the narrative.

What Tolstoy is interested in is not a plot, but the representation of the life process. This is particularly true of *War and Peace*. This chronicle of the events between 1805 and 1815, with its detailed account of Napoleon's invasion of Russia in 1812, unfolds a grandiose social and political panorama and depicts one of the most turbulent periods of European history. Tolstoy portrays 'men of destiny'—Napoleon and his marshals, Czar Alexander I and his generals, including the commander in chief, Kutuzov, who defeated the French. He continually deals with battles and all sorts of fateful happenings; but he seems above all to say that all these presumably 'great' events are but illusions, errors of pride and vanity, that what is really important is the sufferings and joys and strivings of individuals, such as take place in time of peace, in fact that biography is more exciting than history. Thus we arrive at a most paradoxical situation. *War and Peace* is certainly a historical novel and a national epic because it glorifies the resistance offered to the invaders by the Russian people and shows the stamina and the heroism of patriotic effort; but it is a most unhistoric novel in that its author does not believe in historical process and denies any real value to the rise and fall of empires, to movements of millions of men in the wake of battles, victories, and routs. Tolstoy takes a malicious pleasure in debunking the 'leaders' of mankind, in divesting the picturesque of its glamour. His derogatory realism often becomes satirical. Napoleon is presented as a smug, short-legged, plump, and pretentious fool—his nose is runny before the battle of Borodino, and he and his officers believe that his cold has an impact on the issue of the combat. Actually things happen because they follow a preordained pattern, and Kutuzov is wise not to force them and to adopt a passive attitude. Man can be a 'helper,' not a 'creator,' of history; and in order to make his point perfectly clear, Tolstoy even inserts an essay on freedom, determinism, and history into his epic narrative. But in his notion of fiction, he always comes to the same conclusions: basic emotions and the facts of birth, love, and death are the perennial truths of existence, and all the rest is dust and vanity. Events and figures of the past are used by Tolstoy to emphasize that 'true grandeur cannot exist without simplicity, goodness, and truth.'

War and Peace is a family chronicle, or to be precise, a chronicle of three families, the Rostovs, the Bezukhovs, and the Bolkonskys, representing landed gentry and aristocracy. It is a definite apologia for the way of life Count Leo Tolstoy knew and loved, an idealization he felt necessary to throw against the radicals and *rasnochintsy,* who had been busy exposing the wrongs of pre-reform Russia. While he deliberately omitted in his definitive draft chapters that might have shown the more questionable side of serfdom, he ended up by drawing Platon Karataev, a humble peasant who embodied popular wisdom and Christian virtue. But the solid core of this monumental work is the description of the semi-feudal life of the upper classes. He depicted them with such zest and freshness that he transformed dinner parties and Christmas entertainments in the house of the Rostovs or the wild fun of drunken officers or the sentimental love affairs of adolescent girls into visions of radiance and enchantment.

On the whole, the world he recreates here as well as in *Anna Karenina* is a healthy world of sound physical energy and human relations. Even the scenes of battle or the Moscow fire and the descriptions of death are treated with such a sweep of epic grandeur that their horror becomes merely an organic part of a harmonious whole. The general climate is bright and serene, quite removed from Gogol's uncanny masks, from Dostoevsky's criminal pathology, from 'superfluous men,' or from the gloomy atmosphere of critical realism; the assertion of life is akin to Pushkin's.

A master of self-portraiture who used fiction as a means of perpetual confession or self-revelation and accusation, and who made his novels huge milestones of his inner evolution, Tolstoy possessed an enormous power of impersonating and representing other people. Dostoevsky's range, despite the depth of his characterizations, was limited to a few types (especially women). The scope, range, and diversity of Tolstoy's artistic imagination is of gigantic proportions, comparable only to that of Homer or Shakespeare, and his world of men, women, children, animals, plants, and objects is unique in literature. There are 559 characters in *War and Peace,* and all of them are highly individualized, animated by their own emotions and inner strivings and preserving distinct physical and mental idiosyncrasies.

Tolstoy's method of representation is usually labelled as 'psychological realism.' It combines precision of physical and personal detail with the exposition of inner process. The external is rendered visible and almost palpable by insistence on certain bodily characteristics: we are told repeatedly in *War and Peace* about Pierre's clumsiness, the little princess's short upper-lip, or Bilibin's mobile wrinkles.

The psychological is presented in a comprehensive and dynamic way. Every character is shown under different conditions, from various sides, in a 'rounded' way, so that the reader has an impression of knowing them intimately. Moreover, everyone is projected against the background of his environment and his time. Man as an individual is also portrayed as a member of the family and of a social group, within a national and historical framework. No other writer of the nineteenth or twentieth centuries achieves such a completeness on all levels of human activity. At the same time Tolstoy shows the mutations brought about by time and circumstance. All his characters evolve; Chernyshevsky called this method 'dialectics of the soul' because it is based on the fluidity of the personality and (long before Proust) on the most tenuous shifts of emotions. Some of his characters, like Prince André and Natasha in *War and Peace* or Anna Karenina or Nekhludov in *Resurrection,* undergo complete transformations; and as they grow or disintegrate, we follow their changes step by step.

Tolstoy always makes a basic distinction between the way people talk or think of themselves, or are thought about by others, and their true identity. Most of his characterizations are exposures. With sarcasm he tears down the masks of convention and pretence; he ruthlessly detects lies and ambition in those very upper classes he describes with such gusto. This tendency, already present in his works of the first period, including *War and Peace,* became stronger with the years and often assumed the fierceness of wrath. He is impatient with appearances, vanity, or ambition; he wants to bring to light hidden but real motives and true drives, and his psychological disclosures turn into moral judgements. The characters he likes best and depicts with the greatest sympathy are the seekers after truth—Prince André, the intellectual tempted by glory and egotism who discovers on his death bed the law of universal love; his counterpart Pierre, the impulsive 'repentant nobleman' who becomes freemason, mystic, and the potential murderer of Napoleon, and who finally learns supreme wisdom from Platon Karataev (*War and Peace*); or Levin, who after a long period of search and despair sees light through the maxims of old peasants (*Anna Karenina*).

All Tolstoy's works have a moral message, and sometimes it sounds too obvious. The underlying significance of *War and Peace,* for instance, is the opposition of the predatory to the humble, the victory of sincerity over hypocrisy, of instinctive goodness over greed and vanity. Napoleons and Alexanders disappear while the eternal fabric of life—love, family, the yearning for justice and honesty—remains eternal. In *Anna Karenina* the heroine, a beautiful and emotional young woman, leaves her husband and child and is condemned by society because she is completely absorbed by a love affair, a passion which destroys her and drives her to suicide. Levin, the landowner, is saved, for he understands that happiness lies not in the fulfilment of desire but in obedience to the Divine Will. And in *Resurrection* Nekhludov, a rich man about town who has seduced the young girl Katiusha, finds while serving on a jury that she has become a prostitute and is accused of murder; he recognizes his guilt, renounces his privileged station in life, and follows Katiusha, victim of a judicial mistake, to Siberia, where he completes his spiritual rebirth.

Not always are Tolstoy's ideas brought out successfully; in *Anna Karenina,* in *Resurrection,* even in *War and Peace,* the puritanical sermonizing becomes tiresome and irritating. But Tolstoy's religious rationalism is counterbalanced by such poetry in small incidents, such exultation of life, that even those works which most obviously advance a thesis are unsurpassed achievements of representational art. Minor stories and novelettes such as *Hadji Murat,* the story of a primitive Caucasian chieftain, or *Death of Ivan Ilitch,* the poignant description of an average man's agony, or *Yardstick,* a story about a racehorse, and dozens of others, evince the same artistic power and penetrating grasp of the shadings of human psychology.

In the first period of his literary development, which lasted until he was fifty and which included his greatest works of fiction, Tolstoy hailed life and enjoyed immortalizing its fleeting moments. From 1879 on, he devoted himself almost exclusively to preaching and to expounding his ideas. It is usually admitted that a deep moral crisis around 1878 made him change completely. The truth is that it simply brought out and strengthened what never ceased to exist in his mind.

From his early days Tolstoy was marked by contradictions which caused the basic split in his life and work. He came from old aristocratic stock, and he often said he could not imagine himself outside Clear Glades (Yasnaia Poliana), the family estate in Central Russia, with its rambling forty-two-room house, its vast park, and the surrounding cluster of fields and peasant huts, but he always oscillated between the manor and the village, between the traditions of wealthy nobility and the toiling humility of serfs and peasants. At first he led (and later described with delight) the customary existence of the upper classes, but he ended by denying it and by following the philosophy and the way of life of the peasant. Born in 1828, he lost his mother at the age of two and his father at the age of nine, and was brought up by his aunt. He received the usual education of a gentleman of the thirties—tutors, some foreign, the study of French and German, college at sixteen (which he disliked and from which he failed to graduate), then gambling and revelling in St. Petersburg. He entered the army, went to the Caucasus, later fought as a junior officer in the Crimean war against the French, British, and Turks, and became known as the author of *Tales of Sebastopol,* of which he said that truth was their main hero. He had love affairs, travelled abroad extensively, and taught peasant children in a school he organized in Clear Glades on the principles of progressive education. He continued writing with great success but it was not until 1862, when he married Sophie Behrs, a young girl half his age, and settled on his estate that he produced his greatest works. He published *The Cossacks* in 1863 and started *War and Peace* the same year. Ten years later, in 1873, he began *Anna Karenina.* By the time it was finished he became more and more absorbed in his inner moral crisis, of which he gave an account in *My Confession* (1879). This marked his great decision to renounce his past, including his art, and to devote his life to self-betterment and the service of mankind. From that moment on, he wrote fiction either to express his religious beliefs or to satisfy a passion which was stronger than all his logical resolutions.

The change that came over him was the end of a long process. Greatly influenced by Rousseau, whom he adored, and by the primitive life of Russian peasants, he always opposed nature to civilizations and felt that all ills

were caused by society and false values, that man was
basically good. His conscience always worried him. Like
many 'repentant noblemen' of the populist period, he was
ashamed of his wealth and social status, and he endowed the poor farmers with great spiritual wisdom. At
one moment he seemed to have found some peace of
mind in family life and in work as a writer and a gentleman farmer. This lasted, with ups and downs, some fifteen
years, but at the end the sense of guilt and the yearning
for sainthood which underlay Tolstoy's moral search got
the better of him and he initiated his series of great re-
nunciations.

His rejection of the temptations of this world soon became active. Father of thirteen children and a man of
strong virility and erotic temperament, he condemned sex
violently and preached chastity. In *The Kreutzer Sonata,*
an angry tale of jealousy and physical passion (1889), he
hit at the hypocrisy of society which covers up sexuality
with lies about 'love' and affection. Not less intransigent
was his denial of art. He condemned most of contemporary writing, painting, and music as upper-class entertainment, devoted almost exclusively to the themes of
copulation, *taedium vitae,* and pride. He admitted only
works of popular art with moral and religious purpose,
simple, uplifting, possessing a universal appeal, and created for the masses. Whatever he wrote after 1880 was
aimed at fulfilling these requirements. He formulated his
new aesthetic in the treatise *What Is Art?* (1897-98),
which indirectly influenced the critics of the communist
era—who, however, substituted the word 'social' for
'religious.' Since he believed in the virtue of manual labour and the simple way of life, he sat in judgement over
State and society. Enemy of war, of military service, and
of violence, he found no difficulty in showing the dis-
crepancy between political or judicial systems and the
principles of Christian love and mercy. The artificiality
and illusions of competitive existence, the stupidity of
pride and the futility of man's sterile activity were his
favourite targets. Next came the prejudice of the educated class, including the belief in science and medicine,
and the practices of the Church with its pagan ritual and
liturgical nonsense. In *What Is Art?* (and, before, in *War
and Peace*) he laughed at the absurdity of opera and
ballet, and in *Resurrection* he spoke of the Mass as 'words

and 'magic' in such a derogatory way that the Church considered it blasphemy and excommunicated Tolstoy. This did not prevent him, however, from preaching what he called 'true Christianity' based on the Sermon on the Mount and the fundamentals of Christ's Gospel: 'Love thy neighbour' and 'Do not resist by violence.' These two maxims, according to Tolstoy, were sufficient guides for living in accordance with Divine Will. He denied the divinity of Christ and the immortality of the soul, and refused to cope with metaphysical problems, confining himself to morality. This primitive, evangelical religion was bolstered by a few recommendations which reflected Tolstoy's admiration for the peasant: man should dismiss mechanical civilization, live in union with nature, and work manually (Tolstoy made his own shoes and ploughed his fields, deriving from it the pleasure that Levin states for him in *Anna Karenina*), and remain a vegetarian. Simplicity, purity, naturalness, resignation—those, according to the sage of Clear Glades, were the fundamental virtues of man, and their practice could, in his opinion, lead to salvation. No revolution or change of institutions would help; the kingdom of God was within us, and the renovation of mankind could be accomplished only by the reform of the individual, by the concentrated efforts of millions of separate wills.

Rejecting property in the spirit of primitive apostolic communism, Tolstoy went as far as to renounce all his material possessions, his copyrights included. He felt, however, that he fell short of his duty, and at the age of eighty-two he abandoned his wife and children, left the manor of his ancestors, and went as a pilgrim on the roads of Russia. He fell ill during his wanderings and died in 1910 at an obscure railroad station. His remains were buried in the park of Clear Glades.

Tolstoy's life and work had and continues to have surprisingly wide and deep influence. Thousands of his disciples all over the world, from Gandhi in India to Romain Rolland in France, from religious anarchists in Japan to conscientious objectors in America, have followed the moral precepts of the Teacher, while even more numerous admirers have enjoyed the unparalleled master of fiction whose novels and stories have been translated into hundreds of languages. Russians, regardless of their religious and political convictions, see in

Tolstoy the greatest representative of their literature, the voice of national and universal conscience, and the source of spiritual and artistic exhilaration. And since Tolstoy started to write in the fifties during serfdom and died only a few years before the 1917 revolution, his figure most completely embodies and sums up the various phases of Russian culture in its evolution through the nineteenth and into the twentieth century.

14. CHEKHOV

AFTER the assassination of Emperor Alexander II in 1881 and the defeat of the Party of Popular Will, a decade of reaction and apathy began for Russia. The new czar, Alexander III, a heavy, narrow-minded man, ruled the country with the aid of conservative dignitaries such as Konstantin Pobiedonostsev, the head of the Holy Synod, who was suspicious of science and reason, believed in the 'force of inertia,' and tried to preserve the status quo through fear and repression. While the economy and military might of the empire were growing steadily, the autocracy froze cultural and political life. It maintained aristocractic privilege and sharp class division, restricted education, fettered public opinion, enforced censorship, suppressed civic initiative, persecuted national minorities, and introduced 'traditional nationalism' as an obligatory credo. A stifling atmosphere of bad taste and boredom made life, especially that of the gentry and the middle class, stagnant and monotonous, and literature reflected the gloom of the age. No wonder that the dispirited youth acclaimed the highly sentimental poet Semion Nadson (1862-87), whose idealistic, melancholy lamentations corresponded with the mood of the 'lost generation,' and the story teller Vsevolod Garshin (1855-88), a talented, pathologically sensitive writer, who was driven to suicide by his 'sore conscience' and his rejection of 'evil, disgusting reality.' Garshin's portrait can be found in *The Fit,* a story by Chekhov, one writer who was destined to become the most prominent chronicler of his time.

Anton Chekhov, born in 1860 in Taganrog on the Sea of Azov, son of a small shopkeeper and grandson of a serf, had to improve his station in life the hard way. After strenuous school years in his native town, he joined his large family in Moscow, where they were struggling against poverty. A medical student at the age of twenty, he started publishing humoristic sketches under various pen names, mainly to make money. Writing, however, soon became his principal occupation. He gained his M.D. diploma but abandoned medicine for literature. By the age of thirty he was firmly established as a first-class story teller, and his fame kept growing. At the end of the century the Moscow Art Theatre enhanced his reputation as a leading and daring playwright; and when Chekhov died from tuberculosis in 1904, he was mourned as a great national loss. No political changes could ever affect his popularity, and he was as widely read and loved under the Soviets as he had been before the Revolution. During the last fifty years he has also been highly appreciated abroad, particularly in Anglo-Saxon countries, and today he is universally recognized as one of Russia's most significant and influential writers.

Chekhov believed that his role was limited to that of a social chronicler. 'Future generations,' he remarked, 'will not speak of Chekhov, Korolenko, Tikhonov, and others, but will simply call them all writers of the eighties.' It is true that Chekhov knew Russia well and filled his pages with representatives of all walks of society, from peasants to nobility. In his sketches and longer tales he brings forth petty officials, provincial clerks, shrewd tradesmen, dull school teachers, humble priests, and ignorant police officers. His main character is the commonplace man, a mediocre personage devoid of any striking traits who leads a trivial existence. His interests are low, he is mean and narrow-minded, and when he loses at the card table he flogs his son next morning for compensation; he is overcome with joy when the local paper mentions his name in connection with a traffic accident; and when he gains a decoration, he pins it on his lapel and walks the streets in freezing weather, his overcoat open. Chekhov laughs at him and exposes his ridiculousness in anecdotal and farcical situations. In the first period of his work, as humorist and satirist, he enjoyed showing all the contortions and stupidities of those hapless holiday-makers, drunken coachmen, unfaithful wives, betrayed husbands, corrupted policemen, and avaricious merchants. Most of his stories before 1896 (and some even later) are nothing but light revelations of human pretence, droll portrayals of folly and banality. Chekhov, however, grew out of his own facetiousness. In general he offers an example of a writer who never stopped developing and whose horizons broadened continually while his personality increased in depth and wisdom. His work became less frivolous and acquired new dimensions, both in representation and in its symbolic interpretation of reality.

In the nineties Chekhov concentrated much more on the negative, destructive aspects of life than on the comic, and his heroes underwent a transformation. Now Chekhov mostly depicted members of the intelligentsia and of the upper classes. Passivity and discouragement marked the majority of his characters. The so-called 'moody men' of his stories were average citizens who hardly knew what to do with their lives and were resigned to the rut of a dull and meaningless existence. They usually live in some forlorn little town, drink vodka, play cards, listen to gossip, are nauseated by the sameness of days and nights, and lose any capacity for strong emotion or productive work. They are victims of triviality and boredom, and they cannot escape from drowning in dull resignation. Sometimes they are powerless idealists, such as the doctor of *Ward N6* who speaks of Beauty and Idea while his hospital lacks thermometers and his patients are beaten up by a coarse warden. Others shy away from reality by creating magnificent visions, like the hero of *The Black Monk,* who finds happiness in the vagaries of his imagination. And finally some of the intellectuals who have intelligence and education, such as the professor in *The Dreary Story,* one of Chekhov's best tales, are forced to recognize in their old age that their life has lacked a focal point and that they have never learned how to deal with problems of love, loneliness, deceit, and human communication. 'A Russian,' says Vershinin in *The Three Sisters,* 'is particularly given to exalted ideas, but why is it he always falls so short in life?'

Most of Chekhov's moody men become what they are not merely because of their environment and the dreadful social and political conditions in their country—their psychological dispositions make them spineless and sluggish. Some of them, such as the teacher in *The Man in a*

Case, are dried up and dehumanized and repeat empty gestures from habit. Many, like the doctor in *Yonych,* have betrayed their youthful dreams, grown heavy with food and slackness, and accepted boredom and dishonesty as inevitable accompaniments of age and fate. And finally, many of Chekhov's women, like the heroine of *The Grasshopper,* are so silly and flighty that they fail to see the truth and barter true love for false glamour.

It looks at first glance as though Chekhov's characters simply extend the long series of 'superfluous men' of the nineteenth-century literature. Intellectuals who adore words and avoid deeds, who ruin themselves and their families through laziness and lack of conviction in a society oppressed by autocracy and gnawed by discouragement and passivity; harmless eccentrics; frustrated men; unhappy women; lawyers, doctors, teachers, journalists, landowners, and army officers make up the endless procession of Chekhovian characters.

Chekhov's refusal to 'draw conclusions' or to deliver messages, his sober, highly controlled style, his alternation of light humour with serious dialogue, his equally objective treatment of comic and tragic incidents drove critics to a completely wrong evaluation of his stories. Social-minded essayists of his time, such as Mikhailovsky or Skabichevsky, reproached him for the 'lack of an attitude and of moral judgement.' What they missed was this literary form which avoided those very expressions of opinion typical of the Russian realistic school. Whatever Chekhov wanted to convey to his readers he did not by direct statements but by implication, by subtle hints, and by the infectious atmosphere of all his stories and plays.

By no means could Chekhov be identified with his characters. He was an active man whose work was a plea for activity and a glorification of will. In his own words, he believed 'in health, intelligence, talent, inspiration, love, and absolute freedom, freedom from coercion and falsehood.' This sensitive, delicate artist was a convinced positivist and humanist with the ideal of fully developed harmonious individuality. For a while he was attracted by Tolstoy's moral policy of non-resistance to evil by violence, but by 1890, after his voyage to the Island of Sakhalin, a penal colony, he abandoned that doctrine and re-asserted the value of struggle, and a belief in liberalism.

'Reason and justice tell me,' he wrote in his half-joking manner, 'that there is more humanity in electricity and steam than in chastity and vegetarianism.' In *Gooseberries* he challenged Tolstoy's didactic tale of *How Much Land Does a Man Need* by saying, 'It is customary to affirm that man needs but seven feet of earth. That, however, will suffice only for a corpse. A human being needs more than seven feet, more than a whole estate— he needs the whole world.'

Chekhov did not belong to any political party and never showed any radical leanings, but he was one of that vast fraternity of Russian liberal intelligentsia and he shared their code of behaviour and their aspirations. When, by decision of the Czar, his friend Gorky was deprived of membership in the Russian Academy for political reasons, Chekhov, himself an Academician, resigned in protest. He always repeated that 'he who does not want anything, has no hopes and no fears, cannot become a writer.'

Chekhov's main target was the nobility and his fellow intellectuals. This does not mean that his portrayal of the peasants, to whom he devoted two great and pathetic stories—*Peasants* and *In the Ravine*—or the bourgeoisie, who figure in dozens of his tales, was less revealing; it was only that most of his 'superfluous men' by birth or education belonged to the upper classes. In his plays there are many statements directed against the intelligentsia. Trigorin says in *The Sea Gull:* 'The intellectuals seek nothing, do nothing, are unfit for work of any kind,' and Trofimov, in *The Cherry Orchard,* is even harsher. 'They read nothing, have little taste in art,' he says, 'and they talk, talk, talk while surrounded by dirt, vulgarity, and Asiatic backwardness.' Chekhov was ruthless in stressing the defects of the decaying nobility and the re-signed intelligentsia, but he also foresaw with prophetic insight the changes imminent within Russian society, and gave voice to dreams of a better future.

Already in *The Three Sisters* Vershinin dreams of how beautiful life will be in 200 years, and Irina and Tuzenbach talk of useful work to transform everything. In *The Cherry Orchard* the young people, Ania and Trofimov, plan to go to Moscow; they say that 'All Russia is our garden' and have great hopes in 'a higher truth, a higher happiness.' There is the same glimmer of new expectation in Chekhov's last tale, *The Betrothed,* and in some earlier stories.

This note of hope led some critics to the conclusion that Chekhov's pessimistic mood was determined generally by his social environment and that it reflected the worst years of Alexander III's reign. Such an assertion seems, however, inaccurate. Chekhov reflected not merely the effect of a regime. He dealt with some constants of human nature, and the impact of his stories lies precisely in their universality. In his work there are two kinds of futility—the social futility of a declining class, of the discontented intelligentsia before the Revolution of 1905, and the human futility of people crushed by life, frustrated in their hopes, distorted by fate, dehumanized by the cruelty and stupidity of man's condition. 'Masha, why do you wear black?—I am mourning for my life, I am unhappy'—this quotation from *The Sea Gull* could serve as a motto for most of Chekhov's characters. He dealt with standardized people sentenced to a daily routine of repetitious work and mechanized entertainment. One of his main themes is the loss of identity, the lack of communication and authenticity in human relations. This explains the strange conversations between his protagonists in his tales as well as in his plays. Instead of speaking dialogues, they are deaf egotists exchanging monologues.

Another feature of Chekhov's work which makes it lasting and alive today is his approach to psychological reality. His whole attitude toward his characters is based on the rejection of pretence and pomposity. He indubitably followed Tolstoy in his anti-Romantic hatred of sham, tinsel, and bombast, just as he detested rhetorical high-pitched writing. He divests his characters of lies and falsehoods and presents them in essence, exposing illusions, conventions, and dishonesty. His work has the genuine ring of integrity and sincerity, and this clear, pure quality is combined with compassion and irony. Chekhov never raises his voice. He speaks in the even tones of a benevolent observer whose sharp eye does not miss a thing but whose kind heart refuses to pronounce a harsh verdict. No moralist, he simply says to us, as Gorky remarked, 'you live badly, ladies and gentlemen,' and his smile has the indulgence of a very wise man. This warmth, highly appreciated by the Russians on all levels of human converse, gives a popular charm to his work. Like everything he did in his own life, it is controlled and reserved, and as deep as it is restrained.

One can say that this restraint, this sense of measure, came to Chekhov from Turgenev, whose lyrical genius seems so akin to his own. But Chekhov's stories are a departure from Turgenev and from the classical realism. Even though he considered himself a realist and was greatly concerned with the accuracy and precision of his observation, his stories are written in an impressionistic manner and based on carefully chosen symbolic details. They have a verbal rhythm and are composed as poetic rather than purely narrative units. Instead of long expositions, discursive psychological analyses, and large canvases, we are confronted with fragments (Chekhov could never write a novel) in which characters are neither treated in depth nor rounded but are presented in their 'aura,' in fleeting moods and irrelevant conversations. Action is implied or talked about rather than presented, and Chekhovian men and women walk around in 'dressing gowns' and are explained to us through trivialities and nuances. Chekhov said to Korolenko, 'I can only write from memory and not directly from nature. The subject of my story must first go through the filter of my mind so that only what is typical and important remains in it.' But what Chekhov considered important often appears insignificant at first. Through disconnected, inconsequential details and understatement, everything seems to be toned down, to acquire a uniform greyish colour; and his landscapes are mere glimpses, like watercolours in the Japanese manner. And since his tales lack exciting plots and mostly convey nostalgic feelings or subtle suggestions of a hidden reality, a great deal is left to the reader's imagination. The composition avoids climaxes, the story usually lacks a punch, and we are often under the impression that no obvious point has been made. The true meaning of most of his stories emerges only after we have read the last sentence and start thinking about it; and sometimes the delayed effect has all the force of a discovery or revelation. This method, combined with the elegance and simplicity of a carefully polished style, made Chekhov one of the masters of the modern short story, and his influence is felt in the works of many writers, from Katherine Mansfield down to Ernest Hemingway, or Katherine Ann Porter.

Chekhov's dramas, *Ivanov, The Sea Gull, Uncle Vanya, The Three Sisters,* and *The Cherry Orchard,* brought about a radical change in playwriting and were instrumental in the triumph of the Moscow Art Theatre, which found in the interpretation of Chekhov's works a new artistic medium. There is scarcely any plot in all these plays and even the most salient incidents, such as the suicide that occurs toward the end of *Ivanov,* or the one in *The Sea Gull,* or Tuzenbach's death in a duel *(The Three Sisters),* or Uncle Vanya's attempt to kill Professor Serebriakov, are devised as psychological rather than dramatic climaxes. All of Chekhov's plays are built on the relationship between protagonists, and since the nature of these is revealed from the very beginning, nearly all dramatic suspense or surprise is excluded. We know almost immediately after the curtain is raised that Ivanov no longer loves his sick wife, who adores him, and that he is in love with the young girl Sasha. In *Uncle Vanya* the title character tells us right away that Professor Serebriakov is a parasite and an empty pompous egotist, at the same time confessing his love for Elena, the professor's wife. In *The Sea Gull* both the drama of the young actress Nina, whose life is going to be ruined by her love for the writer Trigorin, and the failure of the young playwright Trigorin to win her are fully outlined in the first act. In *The Three Sisters* loneliness and unhappy love are not acted but merely talked about, and in *The Cherry Orchard* the sale of the ancestral estate by ruined patricians does not bring about any sharp conflict but simply gives rise to conversations, recreations, and casual comedy.

It may be said that Chekhov situated the most spectacular events in the lives of his protagonists offstage. He replaced incidents and action with undercurrents, undertones, lyricism, moods. He used transformations of tonality and successive shifts of impression to arouse emotions in his audience. The Moscow Art Theatre enhanced these features by using elaborate settings that gave the atmosphere of the play, by exploiting pauses, prolonged silence, and sound effects (music, axe-strokes, distant noises) as scenic devices. The objective of realistic portraiture was achieved, according to Chekhov, through poetic suggestion; hence the term Lyrical Drama so often employed to describe his theatrical innovations.

While remaining in the main stream of realism, Chekhov's plays and tales absorbed many devices of symbolism and poetic narration and departed from old trends. Their impact on the Russian literature of the nineteenth century was enormous. One can find his mark in the works of a great many prose writers before and after the Revolution, from Kuprin, Zaitzev, and Bunin down to Fedin, Katayev, and other Soviet novelists. This influence has not yet exhausted itself, and Chekhov continues to remain, in the second half of our century, not only a model for imitation but also a live source of direct inspiration.

15. THE MODERNIST MOVEMENT

TOWARDS the turn of the century, three main trends revealed themselves in Russian society. The Empire continued to grow economically. Its industry, its urban population, and its proletariat were expanding; its capitalism and its bourgeoisie were gaining in wealth and weight; and the onslaught of new forces was causing numerous cracks in the old social framework. Storms and upheavals were imminent.

The cyclic development of the educated classes, alternately reactionary and progressive, did not fail to produce, after a decade of dull apathy, a new awakening of liberal impulses. Despite reprisals and persecutions, various brands of socialism spread all over the country, and thousands of secret adherents acted and spread propaganda through clandestine organizations. The populists, however, lost their monopoly. The defeat of the Party of the Popular Will and the failure of several attempts to revive it in the eighties, one of which cost the life of Lenin's brother, shattered populism and destroyed its illusions about the peasant, the role of the rural commune, and the imminence of revolution. A new revised 'critical populism' replaced the old doctrine. It was led by Nicholas Mikhailovsky (1842-1904), an influential writer of essays and literary criticism. His view was that 'the interests of labour coincide with the interests of the in-

dividual who expresses himself in creativeness and work.'
Critical populism, called also Russian socialism, opposed
Marxian concepts of dialectical materialism and of
economic interpretation of social and political processes;
it insisted on the role of the individual and of moral
factors in history, and it formulated the theory of a special 'Russian way of development' and of the particular
character of her inevitable revolution. These principles
became the ideological foundations of the social-revolu-
tionary party, established by the beginning of the century
as a powerful underground alliance of populist forces.
It continued the terrorist tactics of its predecessors, impressed the popular imagination with its spectacular attempts on the lives of Czarist dignitaries and Grand
Dukes, and wrote a colourful page into the history of the
Russian revolutionary movement, filled with blood, heroism, martyrdom, and treason. Its crisis came after 1917,
when, after a brilliant beginning, it was supplanted and
later annihilated by the Communists.

In the nineties the Marxists emerged as successful
rivals of the populists. Their leader, George Plekhanov
(1856-1918), jeered at the populist philosophical idealism, at their 'socialism of the heart, the falderal of Duty
and Beauty,' accused them of 'little bourgeois peasant
leanings' and proclaimed that 'the revolutionary movement in Russia can triumph only as a labour movement.'
The Marxists rapidly made considerable inroads in the
populist 'reserve' (the intelligentsia and the university
youth) and also gained followers among industrial workers, professional groups, and white-collar employees.
Even though a strong group in their midst, the economists, mainly formed by young professors and scholars,
dreamed of 'legal Marxism,' the majority of marxists accepted the necessity of a political struggle against autocracy and covered the country with a network of secret
groups. Their reunion led to the formation of a Social
Democratic party (split into 'bolsheviks,' and 'menshe-
viks' since 1903). Most of the Communist leaders, including Lenin, came from those very circles which were
studying Marx in the nineties and arguing against the
populists about the role of capitalism in Russia.

Apart from the socialists, other liberal groups formed
a less radical opposition to the existing regime, and their
number and strength was also on the rise. The largest

liberal body, the Constitutional Democrats, led by Pavel Miliukov (1859-1943), a history professor and a statesman, had formed a party by 1905. And, finally, a large cultural movement that originated in the nineties had a tremendous impact on the following generations and produced new trends in art, literature, theatre, and education, which carried over into the revolutionary period.

There is no doubt that the artistic productivity, the intellectual searching, and the general atmosphere of expectation and excitement in this period were so amazingly intense and wide that the name of 'the Silver Age,' usually affixed to the years between 1894 and 1917, is justified. The explanation of the phenomenon is, however, less clear, and Russian historians still debate whether this renaissance of arts and letters corresponded to the whole upward trend of Russian life, reflected the European revival of Romanticism, or simply was the last magnificent flowering of a decaying class in a doomed society.

Even though some of the great figures such as Tolstoy were still alive in the nineties, the realistic school was on the decline. Its representatives produced only secondary works, in which the narrative was diluted by dull pedestrian details. Only a few writers kept higher standards. The neo-populist Vladimir Korolenko (1853-1921) charmed his readers with his warm humour, humanitarian faith, and moral integrity; yet his best short stories, such as *Makar's Dream,* and his Siberian tales, as well as his later chronicle, *The Story of My Contemporary,* have a modest place in Russian letters.

The reaction against realistic epigones and the literature of social significance coincided with the revolt of the young who could not accept the tenets of sociological criticism prevalent in all leading monthlies and dailies. Instead of being concerned with social messages and political implications, the poets of the nineties asserted the right of self-expression, and defended individualistic imagination and 'pure art.' Strongly influenced by French poetic trends and often inspired by Baudelaire's *Correspondances,* the Russian 'decadents,' as they proudly agreed to be called, attacked traditional criticism and insisted on a refinement of sensations, artificial paradises of creative whim, and a renovation of form. Their articles and anthologies provoked at first jeers and cat-calls but the modernists rapidly gained many new followers, and by the turn of the century it became clear that the majority of young writers either belonged to the modernists or looked upon them with great sympathy. In the next decade they expanded their influence and assumed comanding posts in poetry, criticism, painting, and the theatre. Diaghilev's ballets, which enchanted Europe and America; the art of Bakst Vrubel, and of the group 'The World of Art'; the music of Scriabin, Medtner, Stravinsky, and Prokofiev; or the theatre of Tairov, Meyerhold, and others, came all from the same modernist movement which, on the whole, was anti-realist.

The first group of 'decadents' who employed new rhythms to express their dreams of beauty, eroticism, fancy, and Nietzschean self-assertion, and who used symbols to hint at a hidden reality distinct from the appearance of the visible world, comprised very different personalities. The head of the movement, Valery Briussov (1873-1924), wrote that he did not recognize 'any obligations save the virginal faith in myself.' He adored literature with all the devotion of a lover. Even though he fancied the attitudes of an orgiastic dionysian poet, his verse was highly polished and cold. He described the madness of the senses, or the voluptuousness of the embrace, but dwelt with even greater pleasure on historical images and on abstract, symbolic concepts. He utilized myth and legend, wrote ballads with Wagnerian overtones, and remained throughout his life a learned servant of the Muses. A scholar, a good linguist and philologist, an excellent student of Russian and French writers, Briussov was a master of form, who 'checked harmony through algebra.' He lacked any mystical experience, used symbols as aesthetic signs of an orderly verbal system (this is particularly true about his ornate historical novels), and really cared only for aesthetic values. His political opinions were always very radical, and after the Revolution he joined the Communists.

While Briussov infused new blood into Russian versification by introducing new, often severe, metres, mostly of classical or French origin, Konstantin Balmont (1867-1943), the Orpheus of the new movement, excelled in highly musical stanzas. He was as effortless and spontaneous as Briussov was laborious and scholarly. The lilting melodiousness of his verse, the enticement of his alternating metres, his sonorous rhymes, his alluring allit-

erations, and the extraordinary inventiveness of his in-
flections, tonalities, and rhythms made him one of the
most influential modernist poets. His work underwent
many changes of mood. He served equally the 'gods of serene repose and the gods of movement,' as he wrote himself; he passed from melancholy to the tempestuous affirmation of love, from outbursts of passion to sweet lyrical pieces, from folklore imitations to versions of Poe,
Baudelaire, Calderon, or Shelley. The charm of his poetry was that of a beautiful cloud, and it passed away as
quickly. The peak of his influence was between 1904 and
1910 when every young poet in Russia was bound to imi-
tate Balmont. His role in the rebirth and enrichment of
Russian poetry was a great one, but already, on the eve
of the First World War, his popularity faded, and he soon
seemed out of date. This 'Russian troubadour' was, however, the last to notice the change. He was very much of
a poetic Don Quixote, and the realities of life did not in
the least perturb him in his incessant pursuit of dreams.
After 1918 he became an *émigré* and died in Paris
during the German occupation, poor, lonely, and forgotten.

Much more complex and 'decadent' were Theodore
Teternikov, who wrote under the pen name of Sologub
(1863-1927), and Zinaida Hippius (1867-1945). They
did not gain the fame or influence of Balmont or Briussov, but they left works (especially Sologub) of a lasting
poetic value. The short, highly melodious lines of Sologub's perfect verse, with their anti-rhetorical precision, so
different from Briussov's oratory or Balmont's verbosity,
appeared simplicity itself but actually concealed a subtly
pessimistic philosophy. Sologub believed that Satan ruled
the human race, and he accepted dreams and erotic per-
versity as the only escape from an oppressive and illusory
reality. But he also insisted on the inevitable defeat of the
dreamer, and often took up the theme of Dulcinea, Don
Quixote's Beautiful Lady of Tobosa, who turns into Al-
donsa, the fat and coarse kitchen maid. Deliberately he
shut himself behind a 'flaming circle' (the title of his best
collection of poems) and, like a sorcerer, performed
weird rites, called up spirits, and made other efforts to
flee from 'the prison of being.' Split between the ennui
of life and the boundless soaring of imagination, he always contrasted frail beauty, symbolized by the slender

bodies of adolescent boys and girls, with the bestiality of men and the coarseness of existence. This theme forms the symbolic level of his novels, of which *The Little Demon* (1907) is not only the best example of Russian symbolist prose but also a remarkable work of literature, a classic whose main character, the provincial teacher, Peredonov, the epitome of vulgarity and meanness, afflicted with a persecution mania, is akin to the old Karamazov and Yudushka Golovlev. Abundant in twists of morbidity and psychological complexes, the narrative blends a realistic study of environment with a dream-like fantasy which reminds one of Gogol. Sologub's later trilogy *Created Legend* (1908-12), despite pages of poetic beauty, presented a mixture of magic and politics, witchcraft and Manichean philosophy, perverse maidens and whipped adolescents, scenes of torture and depraved lovemaking. The fascination of his art, however, cannot be explained as unhealthy curiosity alone. Sologub is a true and remarkable poet, a magician of the word, a genuine 'decadent' who is perfectly authentic in his sensuous despair, his tortuous sexuality, and his hypnotic dreams of liberation by death.

The Black Masses of Sologub took a more spiritual turn in the serpent-like poems of Zinaida Hippius (1867-1945), who married Dimitry Merezhkovsky and who was closely associated with his literary and political activities, even though she preserved her own creative originality. Behind the façade of demonism and negation, this coldly intellectual writer of intimate verse maintained a malevolent, almost vicious ambiguity. Poet of cerebral complexities, of dialectical and abstract opposites, of feelings and thoughts on the verge of sanity, Hippius achieved a peculiar form, bizzare and simple, elusive and mellow. She was also known for her mordant literary articles and a couple of plays filled with psychological *équivoques*. A fierce anti-Communist, she died in Paris as an *émigrée*.

Between the Decadents and Symbolists was Innokenty Annensky (1856-1909), a teacher of poets whose poems on suffering, death, and beauty, often inspired by French symbolists, were a strange blend of poignancy and preciousness, varied and emotionally refined. An outstanding Greek scholar and translator of Euripides, Annensky was also an excellent literary critic in the impressionist manner.

The writers and poets of the late nineties were first of all aesthetes, who asserted the divinity of art and considered the artist its priest, free from any obligations save those of his sacrifices to Apollo and Dionysus. They attacked the intelligentsia for its lack of aesthetic feeling, its asceticism, and its obsession with social and political issues, until it looked as if their revolt were directed against the basic principles of the Russian liberal tradition. But French symbolism and European aestheticism, once transplanted to Russian soil, lost their characteristics and soon ceased to represent a purely artistic trend, assuming instead the significance of a whole system of ideas and general attitudes. Realism was concerned only with the existing reality, with the visible world around it, while symbolism wanted to discover signs and hints of another, higher reality. The search for it soon became the main objective of the younger generation, and their literary innovations were linked with the religious and social tendencies in their time.

This was already obvious in the work of Dimitry Merezhkovsky (1866-1941), who belonged to the early group of rebels but turned from poems and manifestos to tendentious novels and philosophical treatises. In the historical trilogy which gained him a universal reputation (*Julian the Apostate, Leonardo da Vinci, Peter and Alexis,* 1893-1902), he presented the clash between paganism and Christianity as that of flesh and spirit and hinted at their future merging in the religion of the Holy Trinity. A dialectician, attracted by mystical sophistication and a believer in the kingdom of the Holy Ghost, Merezhkovsky went through different stages in cultivating the religious interest of the intellectuals. Together with Vassily Rozanov (1856-1919), a complex and brilliant writer and a disciple of Dostoevsky, he was active in those Russian religious and philosophical societies which gained large audiences at the beginning of the century. But while Merezhkovsky, despite his talent, remained a cold and cerebral inventor of formulas and concepts, Rozanov revealed himself as a masterful creator of 'human documents' and an original intimate stylist. A nihilist, a sinner, and a cynic who aspired to saintliness and made professions of ardent faith, this elusive man of dubious morality, the author of antisemitic tracts, wrote about the sexual roots of religion and tried to reconcile Nietzsche and the Greek Orthodox Church. As a bold thinker and a profound psychologist he occupies a unique place among twentieth-century writers, and his influence can be traced in most of the decadents and symbolists of his time.

The main source, however, of the religious revival was the works of Vladimir Solovyov (1853-1900), a philosopher, a poet, an ascetic who continued the tradition of Chaadaiev and Khomiakov and who left a profound imprint on many fields of Russian life and thought. Solovyov considered man as a link between Nature and God, and the goal of history the marriage of humanity to divinity, which would overcome the duality of the spiritual and the natural. He believed not only in the individual but also in the collective striving for the Supreme Good, and his mystical philosophy contained the concept of 'sobornost,' or 'congregationalism' or 'conciliarity.' While affirming his faith in the final victory of Light, Solovyov wanted to blend the practical and the ideal and wrote extensively on various political problems. Among other things, he attacked Slavophilism and chauvinism, dreamed of the reunion of churches, namely of Catholicism and Greek Orthodoxy, had prophetic visions of Pan-Asiatic invasions of Europe, saw the next manifestation of evil in Pan-Mongolism, and approached historical issues from a religious and mystical point. His philosophy led to a renascence of Russian theological and metaphysical thought, and later thinkers, Berdiaev, Bulgakov, Florensky, Ern, Elchaninov, and many others, followed in the wake of Solovyov. As a poet he laughed at the modernists and wrote cruel parodies of Briussov and Balmont which were the delight of columnists. But his belief that 'symbols are not an illusion but reality itself' made him write highly symbolic verse, full of spiritual eroticism and eerie allusions.

16. THE SYMBOLISTS

THE second generation of Symbolists, particularly Blok, were greatly impressed by Solovyov, by his doctrine of symbolism as faith, and poetry as the intuitive perception of Truth and God; but the concern with symbolism which dominated Russian poetry, theatre, art, and music between 1905 and 1917 did not stop there. The movement, which started as a poetic rebellion, absorbed the political and socialist aspirations of the intelligentsia and blended their aesthetic with radical and Slavophile tendencies. This new direction was chiefly embodied in the three younger leaders of the movement: Ivanov, Bely, and Blok.

Vyacheslav Ivanov (1866-1949), who left Russia in 1924 and died in Italy as an *émigré* and a converted Catholic, was an erudite man who knew Greek and Latin as thoroughly as Russian. His poems, heavy, magnificent, filled with esoteric hints and classical references, can hardly be dissociated from his philological and philosophical treatises (particularly his *Hellenic Religion of the Suffering God* in which he examined the tragic fate of Dionysus). While establishing a whole mythology of Unity and Multiplicity, Nature and Man, Earth and Sun, Ivanov identified the religion of Dionysus with that of Christ. The highest artistic achievements derived, in his opinion, from the same source as myth and religion, and were collective—epic, tragedy, popular songs, and mystery plays. Differing completely from the aesthetes and Parnassians who spoke of 'purposeless beauty,' this scholar, who anticipated T. S. Eliot and Ezra Pound in his intellectual acrostics and obscure, impeccable, though ponderous ballads, became a spiritual and literary leader. Poets, artists, and philosophers met regularly in Ivanov's St. Petersburg apartment, called 'The Tower,' where the host officiated like a high priest and made oracular pronouncements. King of poets, Viacheslav the Great, as contemporaries called him, showed by 1911 a strong Populist and Slavophile bent; he believed in Russia's particular development, her rejection of the Western middle-class tradition, her cultural and religious mission.

These tendencies became much more pronounced in the work of Andrei Bely, whose stylistic innovations have left a strong imprint on Russian prose and poetry and who is often called 'the Russian James Joyce.' Boris Bugaev (1880-1934), who wrote under the pen name of Andrei Bely ('White'), son of a Moscow professor of mathematics, joined the Symbolists at twenty and wrote poems and novels which provoked a stir between 1903 and 1917. His allegiances were many and militant. A disciple of Solovyov and a friend of Blok, he began as a mystic, later showed strong Populist and revolutionary sympathies, acted as patron to the Futurists, became in 1913 the pupil

of Rudolf Steiner and one of Russia's leading anthro-
posophists, was considered a 'reactionary symbolist' by
the Communists, but declared himself a Marxist in the
1930's, even though his dialectical materialism coupled
with Steinerian illumination was a very peculiar brand in-
deed. Most of his poetic work was constructed as musical
composition. All his inflexions and tonalities, alliterations,
slowing and accelerating of rhythms, auditory effects
were not simply virtuoso tricks but deliberate poetic experiments backed by a wide scholarly background; his
formal analysis of the work of Russian poets and his
treatises on various aesthetic problems have a distinct
literary value. Even more important was his attempt to
establish a connexion between the Symbolists and the
nineteenth-century Russian literary tradition. He claimed
that Symbolists were the heirs of Lermontov, Nekrassov,
Tiutchev, and Fet in poetry, and of Gogol, Dostoevsky,
and Chekhov, in prose, and in his own poems he raised
these very problems of revolution and of liberalism which
until then seemed to be the prerogative of critical realism.
In his novel *The Silver Dove* (1910), the description of a
crude sect of Old Believers gave him an opportunity for
emphasizing the duality of Russian culture and the rift
between educated society and the masses of the people.
His next work, *Petersburg* (1913-16), went further in its
political interpretation of national problems. Revolutionaries and bureaucrats both represented a collapsing world,
an illusory culture. The spectral capital of water and
granite was bound to disappear into darkness and non-
existence, while the kingdom of Spirit was promised for
the future. The astounding composition of this novel,
which deliberately mixed the real, the symbolic and the
ideological, the symphonic unity of its fragmentary parts,
the blending of fantasy and observation, and the extraordinary linguistic richness of vocabulary and syntax,
often eccentric and challenging, if at times pretentious,
esoteric, and irritating, makes *Petersburg* one of the most
important Russian novels of the twentieth century. Bely's
later works (*Kotik Letaev, Moskva, Masks*) are not less
significant on the linguistic and poetic side, but they are
not as forceful as *Petersburg*, which was a great land-
mark of pre-revolutionary prose. At the beginning of the
1917 Revolution, Bely's populism took the form of revolutionary messianism and he spoke of Russia mounting

the Gologotha of sufferings for the redemption of mankind. Even though the work of Bely and particularly his ideas may appear chaotic and at times beyond rational comprehension (especially his exploration of pre-natal experience), this puzzling and disconcerting writer did act as the promoter of a stylistic revolution and of the 'poetization of prose.' He is to Russia what Joyce and Proust were to the West in the twenties, and he ushers in a new era, the development of which was interrupted by the Revolution.

Of a different kind is the change initiated by Alexis Remizov (1877-1957), who was very close to the Symbolists and used their techniques in his prose, but who initiated an original style, striving for a 'national form' based on folklore and popular speech, avoiding the 'genteel tradition' of Karamzin and Turgenev and concentrating his unusual verbal skill on the creation of a truly Russian style often derived from eighteenth-century documents and literature. His work is a maze of involved patterns, linguistic tricks, onomatopaeic play, and grammatical *tours de force*. He shifts from lyrical to colloquial, from pathetic to comic; and in his ornamental prose, there is a weird sense of humour and a high degree of sensitivity for human sufferings. Disciple of Gogol and Dostoevsky, he only hints at religious and moral problems which form the core of his work; but at the same time, like Bely, he imposes style upon reality, he is interested not in the representation but in the transformation and theatricalization of life, he resorts to the fairy tale, the dream, the grotesque, the whimsical flight, and the explosive displacement of fantasy. A strange world of human creatures and ghosts, hobgoblins and animals, simpletons and mythical beings is created by this 'magus of the word'; but his odd visions, however surrealistic, never lose some earthly substance and obey the laws of a measured and highly organized art. Even though Remizov is more respected than loved by the public at large, who refer to him as 'a writer for writers,' he is, after Bely, the most original Russian novelist of the last fifty years. He published a great deal before the Revolution (the novels, *The Pond, Sisters in the Cross,* the stories, *The Fifth Pestilence,* etc.), and continued writing after 1921 as an *émigré* (*Flaming Russia, On a Field Azur, Olia,* some thirty-odd volumes). His work greatly influenced most of the neo-realist Russian writers—A. Tolstoy, Zamiatin, Bulgakov, Pilniak, and many others—before and after the Revolution.

The Russian Symbolist movement reached its peak— and its conclusion—in the person of Alexander Blok (1880-1921). Blok was the son of a law professor and the grandson of a scientist who was rector of the University of St. Petersburg. He was born into a highly cultured and refined group of the Russian intelligentsia and was brought up in the atmosphere of music, literature, and the fine arts. Under the influence of Solovyov and Symbolism, the young Blok blended his religious leanings and his love for Liubov Mendeleyeva, daughter of the famous chemist, in *Verses about the Lady Beautiful*, a subjective and enchantingly musical collection of several hundreds of love poems. When published in 1904, they were acclaimed by the Symbolists (among them Andrei Bely) as a mystical hymn to Sophia, the Eternal Wisdom who was transmuted into Eternal Love; sophisticated critics interpreted the radiance and hidden meaning of each stanza. Common readers, however, appreciated the emotional charm of this lyrical diary, and were captivated by its transparent beauty, and Blok rapidly became one of the most beloved and widely read Symbolist poets.

But while his friends saw in him the Ariel of the movement, an emotional crisis, combined with a crisis of conscience, upset his entire way of life. During the stormy days of the 1905 Revolution and its ensuing political reaction, he awoke to a hideous world of pain, suffering, and injustice. Instead of the Lady Beautiful he met prostitutes, and instead of fairy castles he found himself on the pavements of cities, in front of factories and barracks. His idealistic dreams crushed by the coarseness of life, he expressed his despair in poignant and bitter ballads. Life appeared to him as a Punch-and-Judy show, a pointless children's play, and he wrote of disharmony, vile bodies, and bloodless hearts. His 'prophetic boredom' and melancholy verse, akin to Lermontov's, expressed the frustrations of a Romantic. But Blok had too much passion and vitality to become entirely negative. At first he looked for a way out in dissipation, demonism, and the wild expenditure of energy which produced collections like *The Masque of Snow,* and later *Harps and Violins* and *The Frightening World*. This period of tempestuous loves, Blok's 'precipice of evil,' was soon replaced by one of growing interest in problems of life and culture. While continuing to use all the techniques of symbolism, Blok became the poet of Russia. His love for his country and its people acquired the same accents of mystical exaltation as his *Verses about the Lady Beautiful.*

Populism and Radicalism, with occasional Slavophile accents, coloured his new poems, including the magnificent *Verses on Russia,* and the poem *The Kulikovo Field* on Russia's character and destiny. The premonition of impending catastrophe gave prophetic overtones to his ballads and plays, and in his articles he announced the beginning of a new historical era. The Revolution of 1917 seemed to him the fulfilment of his expectations, and he greeted it with genuine enthusiasm. In his famous poems— *The Scythians,* in which he examined the opposition between the West and the East, and particularly in *The Twelve,* at the end of which Jesus Christ appears as the leader of twelve Red Guards who go plundering and murdering through a snow blizzard—Blok showed how completely he accepted the Revolution, and provoked a storm of controversy. But his support of the new regime was of short duration. He could not help seeing all the blood and filth of the upheaval, and his faith was badly shattered. Confronted with outbursts of violence and hatred, with civil war and governmental terror, and, on top of all, with the lack of artistic freedom, he wilted like a rare plant, fell ill, suffered fits of mental depression, and died in 1921, a broken man.

This tormented poet, with his unresolved conflicts and his duality, expressed the aspirations of the old intelligentsia as well as the tragedy of his own generation. He embodied Russian nineteenth-century culture, he represented its last flowering and its sense of doom, and he terminated a cycle begun by Pushkin. Pushkin, the poet of Peter the Great and of the Empire, is harmonious and tends toward unity and proportion, toward Apollonian clarity; but Blok, the split poet of a critical period, is torn between two Gods, and senses the imminent collapse of the world to which he belongs. Standing at the crossroads of two epochs, he tries to listen 'to the music of the revolution' but is crushed by the cataclysm he wishes to welcome.

The impact of his poetry was enormous. It united in its

stream various currents of Russian thought, from Populism and messianic Slavophile faith to the sense of guilt of the repentant nobleman, from the religious aspirations of former aesthetes to the social traditions of the realists. In his style he merged the poetic refinements of the Symbolists, and all the formal renovations in Russian verse, with the 'low trend' of popular poetry, including gypsy romance and folklore ballad. In *The Twelve* the musical unity of the narrative is achieved through the merging of racy 'quatrains of the street' with highly polished lines.

Blok, the Romantic, the civic poet, the bard of the revolution and of Russia, the mouthpiece of the intelligentsia and of the old culture, Blok, the Symbolist and the 'bearer of rhythm,' is the last great Russian poet of the twentieth century, and the passing of time only adds to the magnitude of his work. He ranks with such luminaries of Russian poetry as Pushkin, Lermontov, Tiutchev, Fet, and Nekrassov.

Symbolism in poetry reached its height in the work of the 'second generation' of which Blok is the most representative. But he himself took to new paths, and he witnessed during his lifetime the growing reaction against Symbolism.

The anti-symbolist movement found its ideologists and its poetic expression in the years preceding the collapse of the Czarist empire. Young people who had been formed in Symbolist chapels began to establish their own groups with new objectives and directions. Michael Kuzmin (1875-1935) opposed his 'Beautiful Clarity' to Symbolist vagueness and gravity, followed Epicurus in philosophy and Mozart in music, and wrote charming, emphatically colloquial poems which aimed at rendering the 'spirit of trifles.' Together with some painters and musicians, he excelled in period imitations and stylizations of the early Byzantine and of the eighteenth century, and his work, light and precise, offered an amazing mixture of aestheticism, pose, and deliberate simplicity.

While Kuzmin and his friends were definitely Westerners, a group of peasant poets, under the patronage of Blok and Serghei Gorodetzky (born 1884), started some sort of Populist revival. They opposed Symbolist abstractions and Westernism with purely Russian themes and popular rhythms. Nicholas Kluyev (1887-1937) did express in his highly interesting and at times brilliant poems the mentality and aspirations of the 'muzhik'; but his literary career was broken by the persecutions under the Soviet regime, and he perished in exile. The influence of Serghei Essenin, another peasant poet, went beyond that of the group and belongs to a later period.

Since 1911, the chief rivals of the Symbolists were united in the group of 'Acmeists' (from the Greek 'acme' the point of highest achievement). 'Art is solidity, firmness,' they claimed, and in their works the pictorial triumphed over the musical, clear-cut images replaced hints and allusions, words were measured and counted, and genres were re-established. The head of the movement, the St. Petersburg master and teacher of poets, Nicholas Gumilev (1886-1921), the founder of 'Poet's Guild,' had two main passions—adventurous action in life, and formal perfection in poetry. From his travels in Africa, he brought poems in which Romantic scenes and exotic landscapes were depicted in well-controlled, precise lines. He praised heroic effort, virility, and the virtues of the Warrior, and stated that 'thought was movement, therefore poets should use verbs rather than adjectives.' He wrote mostly in a major key and celebrated fullness of being, struggle, fulfilment, and a restraint of emotion. His sonorous, at times Parnassian verse has a brassy quality; yet in his best poems, such as 'The Last Trolley,' he also showed, next to verbal clarity, a high degree of intuitive imagination and delicate sensitivity.

In 1921 Gumilev was involved in a political conspiracy against the Communists, was sentenced to death and shot. This was the first great blow dealt by the Soviet Government to Russian literature.

Gumilev's first wife, Anna Gorenko (born 1888), who wrote under the pen name of Akhmatova, became one of the most beloved Russian poets of the first quarter of the century. In her epigrammatic short poems, in her neat and sharp sentences, she told the intimate thoughts and emotions of a woman who alternates between sin and atonement, carnal passion and spiritual fervour. Written with the greatest reserve and understatement, her articulate and expressive verse had an enchanting timbre, a highly moving intimacy of diction. She wrote very little under the Soviet regime, but this did not save her from brutal and unjust persecution.

The most important poet among the Acmeists was Ossip Mandelstamm (1891-1942), whose work ranks with the highest achievements of Russian twentieth-century poetry. Trained by the Symbolists, he rebelled against his masters and used severely classical metres, choosing words as a master-builder selects his stones—the title of his first book of poems was in fact *Stone* (1913). Unlike the colourful Romantic poems of Gumilev or the subtly feminine stanzas of Akhmatova, Mandelstamm's poems, with their Greek and Latin reminiscences, belong to the declamatory tradition of Derzhavin or Tiutchev. The impression of majesty they convey is enhanced by his 'poetization of colloquialisms.' While perfectly at ease in parody, or in descriptive, often ironic portraiture of person and place, he rises to true heights in his visions of beautiful forms, amongst them Russia, her culture, and her capital—St. Petersburg. Even though he stated 'I am nobody's contemporary,' Mandelstamm had a keen sense of history, and he felt and rendered the tragic collapse of the Empire and all the world of refinement which went with her. Under the Soviets he had the misfortune to become 'politically suspect,' and there are indications that he died in exile.

The banner of anti-Symbolism was also raised by a group who called themselves Futurists. Striving for a stylistic revolution, they attempted to reject the writers of the past and tried to shock the public by wearing silk top hats and bright orange jackets without neckties or by using unprintable words in literary discussions. But beneath these affectations there was a serious intent. The Futurists, in the crisis of modern culture, were looking for a new idiom, for new forms of expression. One of their former friends, Igor Severianin (the pen name of Lotarev, 1887-1942), offered some linguistic and stylistic innovations to the general reader under the form of neologisms and extravagant (but cheap) verse. The most original of the Futurists, and their true spiritual leader, was Victor (Velemir) Khlebnikov (1885-1922), who wrote poems which are of great interest to a philologist in that they uncover the roots of words and have an amazing verbal richness and inventiveness. Even though he left no accomplished work of art, the role of this obscure, stammering, shy but unusually gifted man in Russian letters is undeniable. Among Khlebnikov's disciples and followers, quite a few made a mark in poetry and prose; but one of them met with great success. The poems Vladimir Mayakovsky wrote before the Revolution (*Cloud in Trousers, The Spine's Flute, War and Peace*) are certainly his best work, and the most significant achievement of Futurism.

17. GORKY
AND RUSSIAN PROSE BEFORE 1917

WHEN in 1898 Maxim Gorky collected in a two-volume edition the tales he had been publishing in periodicals for some six years, his *Sketches and Stories* became a literary sensation. They sold over 100,000 copies in a short time and made their author famous overnight. Maxim Gorky ('bitter' in Russian) was the pen name of Alexis Peshkov, son of a paper-hanger and grandson of a Volga barge hauler. Born in 1868, he had a hard, at times quite horrible, childhood in Nizhni Novgorod (renamed Gorky by the Soviets), and was compelled to earn his living at the age of seven. He had not more than five months of primary schooling, the only formal education in his whole life, and what he later called ironically 'my universities' were his experiences along the banks of the Volga river as a docker, cobbler's apprentice, baker, errand boy, and handyman. A tremendous thirst for learning led him to read an amazing variety of books—he soon became acquainted with the radical ideas of the intelligentsia and was strongly attracted to Marxism. At one moment, however, the violence and poverty of his grimy surroundings drove him to despair, and he tried to commit suicide. After his recovery he wandered across Russia as a tramp and started jotting down his impressions and thoughts. He went through a long and painful journalistic training, was helped in his literary work by Korolenko, and finally emerged at thirty as the Romantic chronicler of vagabonds and tramps. Largely relying on his personal experiences, Gorky depicted the lower levels of Russian society, the *Lumpen Proletariat* of provincial cities, and particularly drunkards, thieves, and wretches of all kinds. What made his descriptions different from traditional realistic 'drawings from nature' was the spirit of rebellion and individualism in his miserable protagonists.

Gorky startled readers accustomed to the sad, grey triviality of the eighties, with colourful and passionate men and women who gambled with their lives, dared to challenge law and society, and were animated by a tremendous lust for freedom and independence. They were far away from the idealized images of the Populists or the passive 'saintliness' of the Slavophiles. Gorky seemed to have discovered a vein of vitality in the oppressed, and since he himself came from their midst, he inspired confidence and offered them a proof of their dormant possibilities. He did not hide the cruelty, the ignorance, and the 'asiatic' instincts of the common man, and his realistic description often had the harsh flavour of pitiless exposure; yet these stories about vagabonds combined an almost Nietzschean exaltation of the individual with the revolutionary spirit. Gorky expressed and symbolized the trend in Russian society which led to the 1905 Revolution. His 'Song of the Falcon' or 'Song of the Stormy Petrel' sounded to the readers (and to the Czarist authorities) like revolutionary manifestos; and his play *The Lower Depths,* produced with enormous success by the Moscow Art Theatre in 1902, was received by the public not only as a picture of human ruin and misfortune, set as it was in a boarding-house, but also as an appeal for freedom, as a plea for man's dignity. The same motives and themes were patent in Gorky's other plays (*The Petty Bourgeois, The Enemies, The Barbarians, The Children of the Sun*), which, despite their dubious literary value, had a success because of their topical interest. The same is true of his novels—*Foma Gordeyev* (1899), a somewhat loose, shapeless, but in parts powerful picture of the rising capitalist class and of the downfall of a truth-seeker crushed by the Bosses, and *The Three of Us,* a story of three young men, overcharged with scenes of crime and vice and with sharp contrasts between their unconscious longing for the ideal, and the horrors of corrupt environment. In all these early works, along with frequent lack of taste and structure, Gorky displayed great gifts of realistic and dramatic description, and a strange blending of harshness with sentimentality. His interest in beating, flogging, torture, and physical pain was almost akin to Dostoevsky's (whom he hated), and the crudeness of details and thickness of 'life material' connected him with the 'writers of the soil.'

Gorky's close association with the revolutionary movement was the cause of his being arrested several times and made him an *émigré* after the 1905 Revolution. It also gave his work a special character, at times a political tinge, especially when he expressed in his plays and stories his grudge against 'soft intellectuals' and 'hesitant liberals.' A socialist, a friend of Lenin and future Communist leaders, Gorky soon became the figurehead of left wing or proletarian literature. *Mother,* one of his weakest and most popular novels, was the culmination of his 'social message' writing. This story of Pavel, an intrepid and virtuous revolutionary persecuted by the police about the year 1900, and Nilovna, his illiterate and religious mother who gradually rallies to the socialist cause because of her Christianity, and finally becomes a true militant martyr for freedom, is written in a high pitched prose which often sounds flat and artificial. *Mother* lacks the usual vivid characterization present in almost every work by Gorky; except for Nilovna herself and a couple of secondary figures, the characters are schematic and their speeches plunge into bathos. As in the case of *What Is to Be Done?* by Chernyshevsky, the success of this novel is due to extra-literary reasons. The first sympathetic description of revolutionaries, it became a model for many further books on the same theme, and it started a long series of what may be called 'novels of faith.' Ecstatic, emotional, occasionally wrathful, it is addressed to the followers of a new religion and therefore established a pattern which later was piously followed by Communist novelists.

Mother ends the first turbulent and Romantic period of Gorky's activity as a writer and revolutionary. Many critics in Russia were inclined to consider him finished, and spoke of him as if he were dead. Gorky, however, matured in exile (he lived for many years in Italy and did not return to Russia until 1914) and wrote there his most important novels. Some of them, like *Confession* and *Summer,* depicted peasants who wandered in search of truth and faith, and the symbolic and religious flavour of these books provoked the ire of Lenin. Others, such as *The Small Town of Okurov,* or *The Life of Matthew Kozhemiakine* (1910-11), were panoramas of Russian provincial life, with all its poverty, cruelty, and boredom. In these plotless narratives as well as in his three autobiographical novels, of which *Childhood* (1913), together with *Reminiscences,* can be called his masterpiece, Gorky asserted himself as a realist who emphasized the critical side and the national aspect of the great tradition. The work of the last twenty-five years of his life was a panorama of pre-Revolutionary Russia based on recollections and personal observation: Gorky was devoid of imaginative inventiveness. His works were representational 'transcripts of reality,' illuminated by indignation or love; he stuck to 'facts' even though he interpreted them in the light of humanism and high ideals. This transcript took various forms—he wrote successful short stories, memoirs (*In the World,* 1916, *My Universities,* 1923), and a family novel (*Artamonov's Business,* 1925), which presents the development of the Russian capitalist class through three generations and which, despite its lack of proportion, contains memorable descriptions and characterizations. His last plays about merchants caught by the Revolution (*Egor Bulychev and Others,* 1932) have some crude power, but his *Klim Samghin,* a four-volume historical chronicle of Russian life between 1880 and 1917, is an artistic failure, even though some separate chapters and individual character sketches in this fragmentary and shapeless work are amongst the best specimens of realistic writing.

Ideologically and artistically, Gorky belonged to the main stream of Russian classical literature. A national writer concerned with the sufferings of his people and the destiny of his country, he shared the social utopianism and compassion of his great predecessors, and considered his art a service to mankind. Completely unmetaphysical, he displayed a strictly positivistic bent and a faith in progress which came directly from the sixties. As a writer with social concerns, as a representative of the popular masses, as a self-made man, and as the poet of rebellion and labour, Gorky naturally formed a bridge between the literature of the past and writing in the Communist era. The whole generation of young writers brought up under the Soviets saw in him a teacher and a master of socialist realism.

His relationship with the Communists, however, was not so simple, and until 1928 he maintained a critical and at times inimical attitude towards their tactics, and particularly towards their intransigence and terrorism. He preferred to stay abroad and from 1921 until 1928 lived mostly in Italy. Only in 1928, yielding to strong pressure from Moscow, did he decide to return home and to offer support to the new regime. Acclaimed as the great man of letters, laden with honours and privileges, he became the 'Pope of Russian Literature' as he used to call himself ironically, and he wrote articles and made speeches to influence hesitant intellectuals and to win them over to the regime. This was not as simple and smooth as Soviet historians pretend, but the whole truth about Gorky's last years will be known only in a distant future, when documents and facts become available for critical analysis. Although Gorky was called, with Stalin, the father of socialist realism, he never wrote a single story about post-revolutionary Russia—all his work stops short at 1917.

Gorky's place in Russian literature is often questioned by aesthetic critics because of his obvious deficiencies of style and composition and his artistic crudity. Of course, his novels often lack taste or a sense of unity and fitness; but it would be useless to deny the vitality and power of his writing. Its merit lies in its richness of detail, in the variety and raciness of dialogue, in the bold strokes in character portrayal, and, above all, in the genuine quality of his faith, in the Romantic sweep of his 'religion of man.' He is often hailed as the creator of a new literary type; and at least his hobos and rebels were a welcome change from weak intellectuals and repentant noblemen. But his main importance lies in the fact that he represented the realistic tradition in an epoch when symbolism was gaining new and ever-growing audiences, and rejuvenated realistic writing in the twentieth century, after it had declined from sheer exhaustion. In 1902 he became head of the publishing house 'Knowledge,' known all over Russia for its literary almanacs. Inside their green covers one could find stories, plays, and novels by the most popular realistic writers. Some of them were members of 'Gorky's school'; others showed more independence, such as Alexander Serafimovich (Popov) (1863-1949), who later won recognition as the author of The Iron Stream (1924), a novel of civil war acclaimed by the Soviet critics; or Vikenty Smidovich-Veressaev (1867-1946), whose Notes of a Physician was a best seller and whose montage-biographies enjoyed great success; or Eugene Chirikov (1864-1937), the author of rather sentimental novels and plays, who died an *émigré,* or Semion Yush-kevich (1868-1937), the popular playwright and chron-icler of the Russian Jews.

Much more important was Alexander Kuprin (1870-1938) whose natural force and gift for spontaneous story telling gained him a host of admirers. Kuprin lacked depth or ideological vision, but he had some intuitive wisdom and he could write excellent narratives about simple-minded people, such as fisherman (*Lystrigones*), wrestlers (*At the Circus*), sailors and poor musicians (*Gambrinus*). His tales of animals (*Emerald*—the story of a racehorse) are remarkably good. Whenever he wanted to be sophisti-cated, however, he lapsed into cheap sentimentality (his *Sulamith* or *The Bracelet of Garnets* or *Yama the Pit*), but he left masterly descriptions of port taverns, brothels, beer halls, of men with red blood, of feats of physical prowess and professional skill, of artisans, jockeys, acro-bats, hunters. Kuprin became famous after the success of *The Duel* (1905), a novel in which he depicted the empty life of a provincial garrison and an idealistic young officer, a variation of the 'superfluous man.' His popularity as a story-teller grew steadily, and some of his tales such as *Captain Rybnikov,* depicting a Japanese spy masquerading as a Russian officer, are of high quality. In 1923 Kuprin joined the *émigrés* in Paris but felt uprooted. His work declined, and a year before his death he returned to the Soviet Union.

A far more important and complex writer was Ivan Bunin (1870-1953), the first Russian to win a Nobel Prize in literature (1933). His stories, his down to earth pessi-mistic portrayal of the peasants (*The Village,* 1909) or the disintegrating landed nobility (*Dry Valley,* 1911), estab-lished his reputation as an accomplished stylist. His short stories published between 1912 and 1916 (*The Chalice of Life, Brethren, Gentleman of San Francisco, The Dreams of Chang*) contributed to his international reputation. In 1920 he left Russia as a resolute enemy of the Communists and lived in France until his death. As an *émigré,* he published important novels like *Mitya's Love, The Life of Arseniev, Lika,* and many beautiful stories—'The Sun-stroke,' 'Elaghin's Affair,' the collection of tales, *Dark Alleys* and *Reminiscences.*

Bunin moved from critical realism in his early nov-elettes to a poetic prose which united sharp precision of observation with an extraordinary verbal gift, and a passionate attachment to life with an almost oriental feeling of futility. Poet of sensations, instinctive drives and recollections, Bunin has the hard brilliance of a purist and the emotional intensity of a nostalgic lover. Even though his protagonists do come alive, he produces characteristics rather than characters, seldom enters into psychological analysis, but excels in the description of moods, perceptions, fleeting thoughts, passing impressions, and in the painting of landscapes. His tales evoke a Russia of fields and noble manors, the charm of fragrant gardens, the youthful loves of squires, ladies, and peasant girls—the beautiful sunset of a perishing social class. Of course, all this life material assumes a general and not only local value, and Bunin's hints about the magnificence of the universe and the insignificance of man become his main philosophical theme. Yet he is a writer who looks backward with grief, and fills his pages with hidden tears for a time which will never come again. Anxiety and gloom inevitably follow his fascination with beauty, and the cosmic feeling, the knowledge that everything will be dissolved without trace in the sea of nothingness, throws a veil over all the splendours of this physical world in which he takes such a powerful and poignant delight. The prose of Bunin (he also wrote verse in the so-called 'classical' tradition and took a stand as an anti-symbolist) could be linked to that of Turgenev in its delicacy and lyrical charm, and to the writers of the soil in the racy, colloquial precision of the dialogue and the use of a rich national vocabulary. The artistic finality of his sentences, the plastic relief of his descriptions, in which the flux of human desires and fate is projected against the immovable screen of nature, makes Bunin one of the greatest masters of Russian contemporary prose. All critics concur in this statement; but they debate whether Bunin is a Parnassian, lacking warmth and generosity, devoid of any intellectual or moral greatness, or a lyricist with a burning love for creature and creation.

In any case, Bunin's formal influence on young writers abroad and in Russia was considerable, and his writing found an echo or was imitated in works of a series of novelists, from Valentin Katayev down to the group of 'Pereval.'

There is another writer who belongs to the same generation as Gorky, Bunin, and Kuprin and whose literary career, after a flash of fame, ended in almost complete oblivion. Leonid Andreyev (1871-1919) started as a follower of Gorky and Chekhov, in a realistic vein, but soon revealed his strong feeling for the paradoxical, symbolic, and metaphysical. In the years following the 1905 revolution, he became tremendously popular because his morality plays (*The Life of Man, King Hunger*) and stories (*Darkness, Lazarus, My Diary*), brought to the public a popularized version of symbolism. He also made available in readable form all sorts of allegories on death, the myseries of the universe, and the nature of man. In the years of political depression following the revolutionary defeat of 1906, he expressed the pessimism of a society frustrated in its hopes. His dramatic talent, his dialectical forcefulness, his sense of the nocturnal side in man, his mystical and religious leanings, and his eloquent 'high' style made his stories seem profound and meaningful. But despite the fact that he talked in ambiguous or allusive terms of God, Destiny, Love, Death, and Mystery, Andreyev was a pseudo-symbolist, just as the eighteenth-century dramatists were pseudo-classical. He had recourse to gross exaggeration, and his literary manner was melodramatic and inflated. By a strange irony of fate, what survived from his pretentious prose are a few stories in a rather realistic vein. *The Governor,* the poignant *Seven Who Were Hanged,* the grim *Lazarus,* and a few plays in which he replaced allegory with a rendering of the triviality of existence in the Chekhovian manner. Today his artificiality, his love of monstrosity and redundance appear as an anachronism.

The same can be said of a group of writers who enjoyed a shortlived but at times quite sensational popularity between 1907 and 1912 when educated society looked for literary drugs to distract its attention from the collapse of liberal dreams. In the wake of political reaction after the failure of the revolutionary movement of 1905, novels on sex, on perversion, on physical and psychological gratifications of all kinds, and even on suicide found thousands of enthusiastic readers. Some of the best sellers of the era did not try to disguise themselves, but others had overtones of ideas and of philosophy. Such was the case with Mikhail Artzybashev (1878-1927) who started as a realist strongly influenced by Dostoevsky and acquired a certain gruesome power in his tales about death throes, mass executions, punitive expeditions, and murder. His *Sanin* (1907), a novel about sexual freedom, described with naturalistic detail the adventures of a 'superman' and had an enormous vogue. His other novels, *At the Brink,* for example, presented the same unwholesome mixture of sex, violence, suicidal drive, pessimism, and bad taste. Some readers took Artzybashev seriously and even spoke of his 'philosophy,' but time made obvious the flimsiness and shallowness of his novels and plays.

By 1912, when writers like Andreyev and Artzybashev were on the road to oblivion, a new generation of realists came to the fore. Some of them wrote in the traditional vein, like the highly emotional, uneven, often rhetorical Ivan Shmelev (1875-1950), whose novel *Man from a Restaurant* (1912) was almost Dostoevskian in its compassion for the downtrodden. After the Revolution, Shmelev emigrated and wrote loud and loose descriptions of civil war (*The Sun of the Dead,* 1923) and nostalgic evocations of the past (*The Moscow Nanny,* 1941). Boris Zaitzev (born 1881), a disciple of Chekhov, wrote delicate watercolourlike stories and later, as an *émigré* in France, published novels on the Moscow intelligentsia (*The Golden Pattern*), on fellow *émigrés,* and an autobiographical narrative (*Gleb's Journey*), all permeated with poetic religious feelings, in an elegant but slightly monotonous and pale manner.

Much more important were the younger storytellers, who could all be classified as neo-realists. Despite the diversity of their temperament and style, they all learned a great deal from the Symbolists and felt the necessity of renovating the realistic tradition not only by grafting on it the Romantic humanitarianism of Gorky or the aesthetic perfection and pessimistic brilliancy of Bunin but also by introducing different devices of composition and narration. Some of them, like Eugene Zamiatin, the author of the *Tale of the District* and *At the World's End,* moved toward expressionism; others, such as Alexis Tolstoy, who published a series of highly amusing, grotesque novels about the provincial nobility, or Michael Prishvin, the hunter and ethnographer turned novelist, or Viacheslav Shishkov, a regionalist, a humorist, and a historical novelist, or Sergheyev-Tsensky, recently liberated from Symbolist allegiances, and a host of minor storytellers, play-

wrights, and novelists, set out to depict reality but were
not satisfied by the manner of their predecessors. They
used a more complex structure and impressionistic devices
of composition, often took to parody, grotesques, and the
poetization of trivialities, mixed literary language with colloquial and regional speech, and in general accepted all
the verbal innovations of the Symbolists and the 'writers
of the soil.' A breath of forests, black earth, rivers, and
steppes came with them into literature, announcing the
imminence of future change.

18. LITERATURE
OF THE REVOLUTION

THE Revolution of March 1917 and the overthrow of
Czarism ended a thousand-year-long period in Russian
history and began a completely new era. A few months
later, the seizure of power by Lenin and Trotsky and the
establishment of the Soviet regime marked the opening of
the Communist experiment. This event had not only portentous consequences for all the world and for Russia's
economic, social, and political life; in the more restricted
area of national culture, it brought about a completely new
situation.

At first the effect of the Revolution was a negative one.
In the years of military communism, with the terror of its
civil war which cut the country into isolated provinces,
with starvation and the terrible drop in living standards,
literary activity was minimal, and in the subsequent great
transformation of the State structure, cultural interests and
the artistic life were suddenly suspended. Monthlies and
weeklies disappeared, publishing houses closed, the book
trade dropped by 1920 to a mere 2,000 titles, mostly political pamphlets, newspapers became party sheets, academic studies were completely upset, and literature and
the arts appeared about to vanish from the Soviet republic.

The majority of well-known authors, from Bunin
and Kuprin to Zaitzev and Shmelev, from Balmont and
Andreyev to Merezhkovsky and Remizov, left the country
and joined the *émigrés* or, like Gorky, lived abroad
in isolation. At one moment, it seemed as if Paris, Prague,
or Berlin sheltered a greater number of Russian writers

than Moscow and Petrograd. Yet, amidst ruin and death, literary activities were resumed, and some signs of a revival became evident in 1919.

The rebirth began with poetry. Poets published their works or recited them in cafés, restaurants, and public meetings. They interpreted the Revolution either as a religious epiphany (Bely, Blok), as a peasant dream ('Inonia' by Essenin), or as the expression of national forces (poems by M. Voloshin). Messianic motives, coupled with enthusiastic faith in Communist victory, coloured proletarian poems, particularly those by members of the 'Smithy' group.

Two poets, however, emerged as prominent leaders of this period—Essenin and Mayakovsky. Serghei Essenin (1895-1925), son of a peasant, started as a simple-minded village bard. Influenced by revolutionary messianism, he imagined a rural paradise in which the union of man and nature would result in a Golden Age; and while Communists were talking of Marx and the class struggle, Essenin was writing chants using the religious symbols of the Nativity and Easter. An imagist, he headed a whole 'school' with a large following. His dreams, however, did not correspond to the harsh reality—he could not accept the 'Iron Age,' and his attempts to drown his melancholy and his tenderness in alcohol and love affairs were a failure; and ultimately Essenin committed suicide. He remained the poet of lyricism, of grief, of rebellion and conscience, of individual strivings; and he acted as mouthpiece of the generation which longed for a gentle peace in an epoch of violence and fratricidal war.

Mayakovsky, unlike Essenin, fully accepted that very reality which horrified and saddened the rural imagist. He contended that Futurism, this revolutionary movement in literature, corresponded to the social upheaval in Russia and claimed it should be adopted as the official style of the new regime. Together with other ex-futurists, he supported the Bolsheviks enthusiastically and insisted that literature be used exclusively for propaganda. In fact Vladimir Mayakovsky (1893-1930) devoted his great talent to the service of the revolution and for years wrote topical verse and slogans, initiated offensives against the classics as well as against illiteracy, and preached a utilitarian and social theory of art.

In practice he created a new poetic idiom, using short

broken lines and isolated single words, stressing meaning and intonation, emphasizing word play and auditory
effect, falling back on coarse humour. His oratorical poetry aimed at the 'de-poetization' of the language. It
reverted to vernacular expressions and colloquial phrases,
and it was packed with energy and dynamic metaphor.
The Formalists were greatly interested in his revolutionary verbal experiment, and it did open a new chapter in Russian letters. While Communists extol Mayakovsky for his complete merging of poetry and political
activity, critics were impressed by the volume and
force of his voice, by the amazing power of his language and 'down to earth' eloquence. Yet Mayakovsky
must have tired of making poems on taxes, war-bonds,
cleanliness, and party meetings. Certain aspects of the
contemporary scene, which he satirized in two plays
(*The Bed Bug* and *The Bath House*), must have affected
him badly; unrequited love and severe depression pushed
him to the extreme, and, like Essenin, he also committed
suicide. This, however, did not diminish his wide popularity, nor did it prevent Communist critics making out
of him the greatest spokesman of revolutionary poetry.

By 1921 the ruins left by the civil war, the exaggera-
tions of military communism, the necessity of respite and
reconstruction forced Lenin to launch the New Economic
Policy (Nep) and to make compromises. In the field of
literature this meant abandoning the hope that a new proletarian prose and poetry would suddenly spring from
popular sources, and led to a lenient attitude towards
non-Communist writers, particularly those known as 'fellow travellers.' As a result of this more liberal cultural
policy and of spontaneous releases of national energy,
the twenties became a period of feverish activity. Monthlies and publishing houses were re-established; discussions and literary controversies raged everywhere; criticism and research, mainly under the guidance of For-
malist scholars, was resumed with great intensity; the
number of books published grew steadily; and the spreading of literacy expanded the reading audiences. It was
during this decade that the best and most significant
works of Soviet literature emerged, despite the rigours of
censorship and Party pressure, and that a new generation of novelists and poets came on the literary scene.
The most striking fact of those years was the carrying

over of movements and trends which had blossomed
before the Revolution. Communist critics talked about
a complete break with the past, and of the 'proletarian'
traits in Soviet letters, but in reality, prose and poetry
were following a traditional pattern. The influence of Bely
and Remizov was obvious, for instance, in the works of
Boris Pilniak (1894-1938?), the pen name of Vogau, the
most discussed writer of the twenties, who mirrored the
Revolution in rhythmic novels filled with compositional
inversions, flashbacks, symbolic allusions, and linguistic
experiment, topped with a mixture of Populism, Bolshe-
vism, and Nietzsche. Pilniak hailed the Revolution as the
end of the artificial 'St. Petersburg' period and as a return to the Muscovite tradition, and as an explosion of
anarchical, Scythian instincts, an irrational elemental
surge toward an unknown. In his *The Naked Year* (1922)
and in numerous stories and novelettes, he expanded his
concept of anti-European maximalism, but got into serious trouble for opposing the 'mathematical rationalism'
of the Communists to organic wisdom, and even challenging the Party leaders in the novelette *About the Un-
extinguished Moon,* which reported the death of the Army
Commander Frunze, and in *Red Wood,* which questioned
the industrialization of the country. A few years later he
was either exiled or shot, and his name was banned from
the press. The same fate hit Artem Vessely, another of
Bely's disciples, and the author of a series of novels on
the beginnings of Communism.

Isaac Babel (born 1894, date of death unknown) who
was also 'purged' in the late thirties and disappeared
after 1938, belonged to an entirely different literary
school. A Romantic who played with the contrasts between beauty and ugliness and mixed naturalistic, often
repulsive details with poetic vision, Babel traced the
civil war and particularly the Cossack regiments in a series of stories, *Red Calvary,* which were clashes of
light and shade, a counterpoint of contrasts. The same
mood illumines his *Jewish Tales* and other sketches. The
intensity and originality of his work and his bold portrayal of the horrors of war assure him an important
place amongst early Soviet prose writers.

A strong influence on young writers was exerted by
Eugene Zamiatin (1884-1937), whose realistic observa-
tions were matched with expressionistic experiment in

structure. Master of irony, he represented contemporary events with independence and boldness. His social satire *We,* precursor of Huxley's *Brave New World* and Orwell's *1984,* conceived a future Communist society, soulless and mechanical, in which man is completely and cruelly conditioned. This novel was prohibited in Soviet Russia, but other works by Zamiatin, stories, novelettes, and 'fables,' were published, and provoked the anger of the Communist censors. Severely persecuted, Zamiatin was forced to leave for Paris, where he died an expatriate.

He was the foster-father of a whole group of writers, called the 'Serapion Brethren': they affirmed the freedom of artistic expression, refused to listen to political dictation, and learned from Zamiatin how to write 'with ink mixed with a 100 per cent proof alcohol.' Most of them were interested in ornamental prose, complex formal structure, and involved plot. They all wrote about the Revolution and contemporary life—and what material permits more variety in events and characters, more singularity in human relationship, than the years of struggle, transformation, civil war, and reconstruction? Amongst them, Vsevolod Ivanov, one of the pioneers of Soviet prose, wrote in his exotic tales (*Coloured Winds, Sky-blue Sands, The Iron Division*) of Asiatic guerrillas, and emphasized in an expressive, highly ornate language the explosion of primitive instinct and sensuousness unleashed by the Revolution. Another Serapion was the humorist Michael Zoshchenko (1895ñ1958), author of a series of satiric sketches in which he exposed the absurdities and distortions of the Communist era. Zoshchenko created a highly comical effect by having his protagonists speak in a fantastically mixed idiom studded with 'high falutin' ' words, journalistic slogans, and vulgar expressions to reflect the confusion in their minds. In general, satire was very strong in the twenties, in the brilliant hands of Michael Bulgakov, the playwright, and many others.

Benjamin Kaverin (born in 1902), author of *Artist Unknown, The Fulfilment of Desires,* and *Two Captains,* displayed a great deal of romantic fancy and formal inventiveness. Yuri Olesha (born in 1889) wrote a remarkable novel, *Envy,* in which the problem of the clash between the old emotions and the new positive rationalism was presented through imaginative symbols and psychological analysis. A friend of the Serapions, Yuri Tynianov (1894-1943), a philologist and literary historian, initiated the historical-biographical genre— which had such a success in Soviet letters. His *Kukhlya* (about the poet Kuechelbeker), *Vazir Mukhtar* (about Griboyedov), *Pushkin,* and his tales, particularly *Second Lieutenant Kize,* which inspired the music of Prokofiev and was made into a film, are examples of a happy marriage of scholarship with poetic imagination.

Very close to the Serapions was Leonid Leonov (born in 1899), one of the most important Soviet novelists. In his numerous tales, and particularly in novels such as *The Badgers, The Thief, Soviet River,* and *Skutarevsky,* he dealt with the 'dialogue between the individual and the Revolution,' through deep psychological exploration obviously inspired by Dostoevsky. His prose, long-winded and over-written, with verbal twists and baroque embellishments, has definite dramatic power and is marked by its psychological and ideological complexity. Like Olesha and other Serapions, Leonov accepts communism as a new humanism, a harmonious development of the individual, but is not inclined to minimize the conflicts and tragedies it brought into Russian life.

Between the Serapions and the Neo-realists stands Konstantin Fedin (1892), whose *Cities and Years* was the first major novel of the Soviet period. *The Brothers, The Rape of Europe,* and his later works, *Early Joys* and *No Ordinary Summer* (1946-50) are realistic, following the great Russian epic narrative tradition; yet they evince many ornamental and expressionistic techniques and devices. It was Fedin's concern to be the chronicler of his time; and there is a great deal of social observation in his work.

Neo-realists were prominent in the literature of the twenties. All writers who made their successful *débuts* before the Revolution became most influential under the Soviets. Next to Zamiatin, whose activity was curtailed for political reasons, 'the fellow traveller' Alexis Tolstoy (1883-1945), who had at first joined the *émigrés* and then had gone back to Russia, was the most talented. He attained great popularity and was hailed by the Communists as one of the leaders of Soviet letters. His novel-trilogy *Road to Calvary,* of which he published various versions between 1921 and 1941, dealt with the life of the intelligentsia before and during the Revolution and gave a vivid, in part biased, description of the civil war. His writing was uneven—along with his brilliant historical novel *Peter the Great* (1929-45), one of the best of its kind in Russian literature, and excellent short stories, he published popular trash and plays of doubtful value. He had neither the moral nor the intellectual power of the great writer but was endowed with all the craft and temperament of one. He had such a capacity for creating the illusion of life, such an easy facility for spinning a yarn, such an organic talent for portraiture that most of his works, despite their flaws, brim with vitality and suggestive force.

Completely different was Michael Prishvin (1873-1954), whose novel, *The Chain of Kashchey,* and whose stories and sketches about animals and hunters hold an extraordinary feeling for nature and an understanding of man within his organic environment. A pantheist, he is also a master of the language, an amazingly rich stylist, a fine craftsman, obviously close to Leskov and Remizov. One of his followers, Konstantin Paustovsky (born in 1892), emerged in the 1940's as one of the most talented Soviet post-war novelists.

In the stream of Neo-realists were also two prominent historical novelists, Viacheslav Shishkov (1873-1945), the author of *Emelyan Pagachev,* and Serghei Sergheyev-Tsensky (1876-1958), whose novels on the Crimean Campaign and on the 1914-18 war had a very wide circulation and popularity.

A middle of the road position was taken by Ilya Ehrenburg (born in 1891), who was at first associated with the *avant garde* and wrote satirical grotesques (his best novel is the *Adventures of Julio Jurenito*) and cynical expressionistic tales, but who later inclined toward 'literature of fact' and concocted vivid but superficial films of European and Russian actuality.

The situation in poetry was similar to that in prose. The twenties of the Nep was a time of experiment and trial, and, next to Mayakovsky's Futurist extravaganzas on politico-social themes, it was dominated by the complex poetic constructions of Pasternak.

Unlike Mayakovsky, Boris Pasternak (born in 1890) refused to become involved in the events of his time and his famous lines, 'I call out in the courtyard, What millennium are we celebrating there?' were quoted to show his political indifference. He always asserted his independence as a poet and claimed a supreme right to free creativity. His poems united Symbolist musicality with the colloquial interjections of Futurism and traditional classical proportion. His lines are clear, his metres precise; but his poetry is different in the way of T. S. Eliot or R. M. Rilke, with whom he has a great deal in common. His metaphors bridge opposing levels of reality, his words are given many layers of meaning, he manipulates surrealistic autonomous images, alliterations, involved tropes; but all his devices, all his prodigious verbal imagination and inventiveness serve to convey what he calls 'the emotional displacement of reality.' The intensity and the newness of his poems and their intellectual depth make for Pasternak a unique place in Russian letters. His influence was profound and most beneficial—the impact of his dynamic and highly imaginative form can be found in the works of dozens of Soviet (and *émigré*) poets. Yet Pasternak's position in the Soviet Union was precarious. After his first collections (*Above the Barriers, Life My Sister, Themes and Variations, The Year 1905, The Second Birth*), he could publish between 1933 and 1943 only his translations of Shakespeare and was forced into silence again between 1945 and 1956.

After Stalin's death Pasternak wrote *Doctor Zhivago,* a novel representing the fate of an intellectual crushed by the revolution. This extraordinary narrative encompassed thirty years of Russian life and portrayed some sixty characters. The spirit of independence, freedom and religious wisdom which pervaded its pages and its general anti-Communist tendency made the publication of *Doctor Zhivago* in Soviet Russia impossible. It appeared, however, in translations all over the world and soon became one of the most widely read books of our time. In 1958 Pasternak was awarded the Nobel Prize for literature but was compelled to renounce it because of a violent campaign launched against him by Communist organizations.

Second to Pasternak is Marina Tsvetayeva (1892-1941), who emigrated in 1921, returned to Russia in 1939 to join her husband, and committed suicide during the war in most tragic circumstances. Impetuous, passionate, dynamic, she wrote in a telegraphic style; her exclamatory poetry, with its sharpness and accented diction, bears some resemblance to Mayakovsky's style, although the spirit of her work is closer to that of Bely and Pasternak. Besides, she is attached to the Russian folklore tradition. Her romantic pieces, her stormy lines, her plays in verse, and her bizarre prose are like a torrential stream, a single flow of exceptional strength; and future generations will undoubtedly discover her work with astonishment and gratitude.

Among Soviet writers of lesser calibre are other Romantics—Edward Bagritsky (1895-1935, Dziubin), author of ballads and translator of Coleridge, Scott, and Burns; Nicholas Tikhonov (born in 1897), one of the Serapions, strongly influenced by Gumilev, who glorified courage, virility, and loyalty in his terse poems of civil war and revolution; Semion Kirsanov (born in 1906), and Nicholas Aseyev (1889), who both started as Mayakovsky's disciples, later revealing some originality of tone and composition; and Ilya Selvinsky (born in 1894), who led the 'constructivist' group towards industrial and practical poetry but was distinguished in his purely formal innovations of melody and rhythm.

By the end of the twenties all innovations in poetry, except those made by Mayakovsky, were held politically suspect, and the necessity for civic and representational verse was proclaimed from Party headquarters. Poets had to write about current events in a simple descriptive form, and this resulted in a number of lengthy narratives, mostly novels in verse or detailed descriptions of characters and environment. Most of them degenerated into boring naturalistic sequences and artificially optimistic pseudo-poetic chatter. Today one can simply state that all this movement did not produce a single work of value or a single poet of stature.

In general, the opposition of 'realists' to 'modernists' formed the main source of controversy in the twenties and was the matter of political debate and Party decision. While most of the writers of the period had been connected with pre-Revolutionary stylistic trends and were greatly interested in verbal innovations and compositional experiments, the Communist novelists and critics took a negative attitude towards experimentalism and modernism. By 1928 it became clear that even though the 'fellow travellers' wrote about contemporary Russia, their concern with form and their uncatholic interpretation of the Revolution was provoking a strong opposition within the Party and on its periphery. Those who claimed to express the true social aspirations of the new regime ranged from psychological realists to partisans of factual realism. The first announced their attachment to the great Russian tradition, the others affirmed that communism required a politically aggressive and ideologically consistent representation of reality. In the struggle between the two factions, the psychological realists achieved spectacular literary successes, particularly in the person of Mikhail Sholokhov (born in 1905), whose *The Quiet Don* (1928-1940), a lengthy epic of Cossack life before the Revolution and during the civil war, sold more than five million copies and qualified as a Soviet classic.

Sholokhov's merit lay not only in his vivid scenes, his solid portraiture and his comprehensive picture of the historical background: his heroes and their destinies expressed the drama of a whole generation, and the monumental work describing their adventures will remain as one of the most complete fictional documents of the revolutionary era. Sholokhov's novel on collectivization, *The Virgin Soil* (1932-33), written in the same broad realistic manner, is interesting but lacks the sweep and colourfulness of his masterpiece.

Close to Sholokhov stands Alexander Fadeyev (1901-56), whose novel *The Rout* (1927, *The Nineteen* in English) is a moving tale of a Red detachment encircled by the Whites in Siberia. It lacks the epic quality of Sholokhov's novel but is a gripping dramatic narrative, perhaps one of the best in the abundant literature of the civil war.

By the end of the twenties Nep gave way to a new Communist programme which included the forced introduction of *kolkhozes* into the villages, the industrialization of the country through five-year plans, and a more strict Party policy. This encouraged the partisans of 'factual realism,' who wanted literature to be 100 per cent Communist and a tool for helping the government in its endeavours. As models of successful writing of this kind they quoted *Chapayev* by Dimitry Furmanov (1891-1926), an account of civil war, and *Cement* by Fedor

Gladkov (1883-1958), a picture of reconstruction, even though impressionistic in style.

The idea of a representational art, Communist in content, realistic in form, which would reflect the problems of labour, industrial production, and socialist competition was particularly sustained by the Association of Proletarian Writers. This influential group, a sworn enemy of Symbolists and Formalists, exerted strong pressure to turn all Soviet prose and poetry into mere reports on changing social-economic conditions. Novels on the five-year plan, tales on *kolkhozes* were regarded as the true substance of new Communist art, provided, of course, that they followed Party ideology.

The activities of the Association, supported by some Party officials, led to a tense situation between 1929 and 1932. Proletarian writers and their friends seized all the key positions in publishing houses and in the censorship. Persecutions, arrests, and exiling of 'subversive authors,' a frantic and disloyal campaign against the 'enemies,' created an atmosphere of fear and sterility. By 1932 the situation became intolerable and Stalin and the Party decided to put an end to this factional dictation and to 'organize' literature from above. The Association of Proletarian Writers was disbanded, and their leaders demoted. The newly established Union of Soviet Writers included 'fellow travellers' as well as Communists, and the Party not only assumed all control over literature but also gave its official blessing to socialist realism. The latter was defined as a 'truthful, historically concrete representation of reality in its revolutionary development,' aiming at 'the ideological education of the masses in the spirit of socialism.' This meant that the writer had to create in a certain form and that the content of his work had to express Communist ideology or at least be in sympathy with it. It also meant that the stylistic experimentation of the twenties was to be stopped and that no variety in style and direction would be permitted. This was enforced by the purges and the Moscow trials of 1936-38, when quite a few outstanding writers and intellectuals fell victims to Stalin's 'terror.' Special emphasis was put on the liquidation of 'formalism,' and the very name itself became derogatory. This dictatorial policy, with its inevitable simplification, brought on a crop of monotonously similar novels and poems on industrialization, always with their 'virtuous Communist hero.' Paradoxically, the best picture of the Five-Year Plan and of the new building and exploration were given not by the representatives of socialist realism but by such fellow travellers as Valentin Katayev, in his expressionistic *Time Onward,* Leonov in his psychological *Soviet River,* and Yuri Krymov in his neo-realistic *Tanker Derbent.* In the thirties there was a return of interest to the national tradition and to Russia's past. New historical novels appeared, and the stabilization of the regime and an increasing 'Soviet Victorianism' revived a flat, puritan, moralistic narrative, often reminding one of the sloppy writing of the 1860's.

It is true that between 1932 and 1941 a number of works enjoyed vast popularity among Soviet readers and were highly praised by the critics, but these bestsellers hardly ever had any literary merit. They were either journalistic snapshots, like Ehrenburg's novels on youth and industrialization, or illustrative documents of topical interest which offered to millions of Russians the pleasure of recognizing themselves. This was the case with novels on the New Hero—*The Tempering of the Steel* by Nicholas Ostrovsky (1904-36), a poorly written glorification of Communist youth which sold six million copies, and the *Pedagogical Poem* by Anton Makarenko (1888-1939), who dealt with problems of education and juvenile delinquency.

While the quality of Soviet fiction was declining, *émigré* literature seemed to reach its peak in the thirties. It was during that decade that older writers like Bunin, Remizov, Shmelev, Ossorghin, Zaitzev, and Grebenshchikov produced a sizable number of novels and stories, and that the second generation of expatriates was very active, mostly in France. Poetry fared particularly well, with such leading figures as Tsvetayeva and Vladislav Khodassevich (1886-1939), the poet of an intellectual and decadent tradition, and a number of young and talented people, among them followers of Acmeism (George Ivanov and, partly, Antonin Ladinsky) and Surrealism (Boris Poplavsky). In prose the expatriates inclined toward lyrical recollections and personal reminiscences. It is significant that the most successful of *émigré* novelists, Mark Aldanov (Landau, 1886-1957) is the author of large historical narratives dealing with the French Revolution (*The Thinker*) and with Russia's recent past. An erudite sceptic,

Aldanov charmed his readers with his intellectual brilliance, his vivid portraits of 'great men,' his excellent descriptions of historical events, and his references to the present.

While Aldanov's style is old-fashioned and discursive, that of Vladimir Sirin-Nabokov (born in 1899) is scintillating, imaginative, and experimental. In his novels, *The Defence of Luzhin, The Gift,* or the Kafkian *Invitation to an Execution,* Sirin displayed extraordinary traits of irony, poetic feeling, and inventiveness. He is the *émigré* counterpart of the Soviet experimentalists of the twenties.

The end of the thirties witnessed a certain withering of *émigré* literature, and the upheaval of the Second World War dealt it a serious blow. The war against Germany and the tragic and bloody ordeal which the Russians had to suffer from 1941 to 1943, when one-third of the European part of Russia, with a population of some sixty million, was occupied by the enemy, led to a tremendous rise of patriotic feelings. The controls over literature were relaxed, and even though the main themes revolved around battles, guerrilla warfare, resistance, privation, and atrocities, or, later, around the successes of the Red Army, the tone and manner of most Soviet writing grew more independent.

In the novels of Vassily Grossman (*People are Immortal*), and Konstantin Simonov (*Days and Nights*), who also wrote successful plays and poems, in Leonov's novelette *The Taking of Velikoshumsk,* as well as in his plays, *Lenochka* and *Invasion,* in a series of tales by minor writers, and in the highly popular *Vassily Terkin* by Alexander Tvardovsky, a poetic portraiture of the average soldier, in poems by Margarita Aliger, Vera Inber, Olga Bergholz, Alexei Surkov, and others, there was an emotional sweep and freedom, an earnest search for truth on a par with the literary production of the late twenties.

Victory, however, put an end to this liberal atmosphere and to what was called the era of 'loose patriotic exultation.' In 1946 the Central Committee of the Communist Party tightened controls and asked for a more strict interpretation of socialist realism. The implementation of the new policy was entrusted to Andrei Zhdanov, whose name marked the whole period from 1946 until the death of Stalin in 1953. 'Soviet literature,' declared Zhdanov, 'neither has nor can have any other interests

except those of the people and of the State. Its aim is to
educate the youth according to Communist principles.
Literature must become Party literature, and one of its
tasks is to portray the Soviet Man in full force.'

In practice, this meant that Soviet writers were warned
against the lure of the West and against the dangers of
formalism. Anti-European and anti-American feelings, in-
cited by the official press during the 'cold war,' and the
campaign against 'rootless internationalists and cosmopol-
itans' had strong chauvinistic and at times anti-semitic
overtones. It led to a wave of repressive measures, the
elimination of a number of writers from the literary scene,
and a complete subjugation and bureaucratization of literary organizations.

This policy produced a uniform and desperately dull
literature, written according to rigid patterns. The representation of Europe and America as 'capitalist hells in-
habited by villainous imperialists and their starving victims' was matched only by a roseate picture of Communist society bent on increasing industrial and agriculture
output and on the cultivation of Party loyalty. Conflicts
and inner struggle were banned as subject matter, and
one novel after another glorified the stalwart secretary
of the local organization or the president of the *kolkhoze*
as models of wisdom and virtue. Only a very few works
escaped to some extent the falsity and drabness of this
period, notably novels by Vera Panova, Konstantin Fedin,
and Victor Nekrassov, and poems by Nicholas Zabolotsky
(1903-1958) and Leonid Martynov. As a whole, the years
1946-53 yielded the poorest harvest in the history of Russian literature.

After the death of Stalin, a 'thaw' set in. Even Communist critics had to admit that the 'varnishing of reality,'
the spirit of subservient praise of the regime and its leaders, the avoidance of real issues, and the reluctance to
face true conflicts had created a serious moral and formal
crisis. Between 1954 and 1959 discussions on socialist
realism showed the dead end into which literature had
been pushed by administrators, and the suicide of one of
them, Alexander Fadeyev, assumed in 1956 a symbolic
significance. Some new tendencies showed in Russian
literature during the 'de-Stalinization' era of 1956, and
many writers, old and young, began to reveal the defects
and complexities of that very society which had been pre-

sented a few years ago as one huge and beautiful fulfilment. Authors dropped in the past have been rehabilitated. The names of such poets as Pasternak and Akhmatova appeared again in Moscow periodicals, and in many
quarters literary revaluation and re-examination has taken
place. It is difficult to judge whether this movement
points to a revival in Russian literature; in any case that
is possible only if the concessions granted by the Soviet
Government in 1957 in separate instances are expanded
into a true freedom for literature and if the dictatorship
of socialist realism is replaced by a competitive openness
on questions of style, aesthetic theory, and experimentation. This implies at least a relative freedom of self-expression for the individual artist and a liberalizing of existing controls, awards, and punishments, which are still
determined through State security and Party stability.
The glorious past of Russian literature, however, makes
us hope that such conditions will be created sooner or
later, since the drive towards them is irreversible and the
ultimate success of the liberating process is inevitable.

BIBLIOGRAPHICAL NOTES

In this book the author has used the same material and followed the same critical method as he has done in his more detailed works on the same subject, such as The Epic of Russian Literature: From Its Origins through Tolstoy *(Oxford University Press, New York, 1950) and* Modern Russian Literature: From Chekhov to the Present *(Oxford University Press, New York, 1953).*

Critical Surveys. There are few critical surveys of Russian Literature in English. For the origins and the tenth-seventeenth centuries see: *History of Early Russian Literature* by N. Gudzy (N.Y. 1949); also good material in *Russian Folklore* by Y. Sokolov (N.Y. 1950). For the eighteenth and nineteenth centuries: *A History of Russian Literature from Earliest Times to the Death of Dostoevsky* by D. Mirsky (London 1927), probably the best work in the field, brilliant, original, in parts highly subjective; also *Contemporary Russian Literature* by the same author (London 1933); the two volumes in one, slightly abridged, edited by F. Witfield (N.Y. 1949). See also *Introduction to the Russian Novel* by J. Lavrin (London 1942) and *The Epic of Russian Literature: From Its Origins through Tolstoy* (N.Y. 1950) and *Modern Russian Literature: From Chekhov to the Present* (N.Y. 1953), both by M. Slonim. The latter volume covers the twentieth century. *Soviet Russian Literature* by G. Struve (Norman 1951) contains a comprehensive bibliography of post-revolutionary works.

Anthologies. Among numerous anthologies the rather dated and fragmentary *Anthology of Russian Literature* in two volumes by L. Wiener (N.Y. 1903) is still useful. *A Treasury of Russian Literature* by B. Guerney (N.Y. 1943) is a good collection; also his *The Portable Russian Reader* (N.Y. 1947). See also *Selected Russian Short Stories* chosen and translated by A. E. Chamot (London, World's Classics, 1925), *Great Russian Short Stories* edited by S. Graham (London 1929); *A Treasury of Great Russian Stories* edited by A. Yarmolinsky (N.Y. 1944), and *Representative Russian Stories* in two volumes edited by J. Lavrin (London 1946).

Poetry. The most important collections of Russian poetry in translation are: *Verse from Pushkin and Others* by O. Elton (London 1935); *A Book of Russian Verse* and *A Second Book of Russian Verse* by C. Bowra (London 1943 and 1948); *Poems from the Russian* by F. Cornford and E. Polianovsky-Salaman (London 1943); *A Treasury of Russian Verse* by A. Yarmolinsky and B. Deutsch (N.Y. 1949).

Drama. For the nineteenth-century drama see *Masterpieces of the Russian Drama* by G. Noyes (N.Y. 1933).

Soviet Literature. For Soviet prose, poetry, and drama: *Short Stories out of Soviet Russia* by J. Cournos (N.Y. 1929); *Soviet Literature: An Anthology* by G. Reavey and M. Slonim (London 1933); *Modern Russian Stories* and *Soviet Stories of the Last Decade* by E. Fen (London 1943 and 1945); *Modern Poets from Russia* by G. Shelley (London 1942); *Soviet Poets and Poetry* by A. Kaun (London 1943); *Six Soviet Plays* by E. Lyons (N.Y. 1934); *Soviet Scene: Six Plays of Russian Life,* by A. Bakshy (London 1945); *Seven Soviet Plays* by H. W. Dana (N.Y. 1946).

For translations from early Russian literature see *Russian Fairy Tales* by A. Afanasiev (N.Y. 1945); *The Epic Songs of Russia* by I. Hapgood (London 1886); *The Life of Archpriest Avvakum by Himself* translated by J. Harrison and H. Mirrlees (London 1924).

167

The Young Hopeful by Fonvizin is in *Masterpieces of the Russian Drama*.

The best translation of Krylov's *Fables* is by B. Pares (London 1926), who also published an English version of Griboyedov's *Wit Works Woe* (see *Slavonic Review*, London, December–June 1924; in general many translations from the Russian are to be found in this publication).

For Pushkin's prose and poetry, see *The Works of A. Pushkin* by A. Yarmolinsky (N.Y. 1936). For Pushkin's life see the biography by H. Troyat (N.Y. 1950). For critical essays, see a symposium edited by E. Simmons (N.Y. 1937); *Pushkin and Russian Literature* by J. Lavrin (London 1947).

For Lermontov's poems, see *Three Russian Poets,* selections from Pushkin, Lermontov, and Tiutchev by V. Nabokov (Norfolk 1944). *A Hero of Our Own Times* has been translated by R. Merton (London 1928) and by Eden and Cedar Paul (London, World's Classics, 1958).

Herzen's *My Past and Thoughts* are translated by C. Garnett in six volumes (London 1924–7); J. Duffy's version (New Haven 1928) covers only the first two volumes.

C. Garnett's translations of Gogol were published in London and New York at various dates. More recent versions of *Dead Souls* are recommended: by G. Reavey (London 1948, and in World's Classics, 1957) and by B. Guerney (N.Y. 1942 and 1948 under the title *Chichikov's Journey*). See also *Tales* translated by D. Magarshack (London 1949). Critical essays on Gogol include an interesting, polemical, and controversial book by V. Nabokov (N.Y. 1947) and a more objective study by J. Lavrin (London 1952).

Goncharov's *Oblomov* is translated by N. Duddington (London 1929); see the writer's biography by J. Lavrin (London 1954).

Most of Ostrovsky's plays are available in G. Noyes' versions (N.Y. 1917–27). *Easy Money* and other plays are translated by D. Magarshack (London 1944).

The best translation of Aksakov is *Chronicles of a Russian Family* by M. Beverley (London 1924).

Saltykov's *Golovlyov's Family* is translated by N. Duddington (London 1931).

Translations of Nekrassov's poems by J. Soskice (London 1920) and by D. Prall fail to do justice to the Russian poet.

While collected works of Turgenev have been translated by C. Garnett in seventeen volumes (London 1919–23) and by I. Hapgood in fourteen volumes (London 1903), there are many good and more recent versions of his novels: *Fathers and Sons* translated by G. Reavey (London 1950) and by R. Hare (London 1947); *A Nobleman's Nest* translated by R. Hare (London 1947); *Rudin* translated by A. Brown (London 1950); *Smoke* translated by N. Duddington (London 1949); *On the Eve* by M. Budberg (London 1950). See also a Turgenev 'omnibus,' four novels and three novelettes translated by H. Stevens (N.Y. 1950). There are biographies and studies of the writer by E. Garnett (London 1917), D. Magarshack (London 1954), A. Yarmolinsky (N.Y. 1926). See also H. James's essays in *French Poets and Novelists* and *Partial Portraits* (N.Y. 1878 and 1888).

The works of Dostoevsky, in C. Garnett's translation, have been published at various dates in numerous reprints. To these standard editions should be added *The Diary of a Writer* translated by B. Brasol (N.Y. 1949) and Dostoevsky's letters to his wife and friends (London 1917, 1929, 1933). D. Magarshack offered a new version of *Crime and Punishment* (London 1951) and of *The Possessed* (under the title *The Devils*, London 1953) and J. Coulson of *Crime and Punishment* (London 1953) and *Memoirs from the House of the Dead* (London 1956). Critical literature on Dostoevsky in English is very large. For his life see *The Firebrand* by H. Troyat (London 1940), *Dostoevsky* by A. Yarmolinsky (N.Y. 1934, revised edition 1957), *Three Loves of Dostoev-*

sky by M. Slonim (London 1957). Critical essays: *The Making of a Novelist* by E. Simmons (N.Y. 1950), *Dostoevsky*—books by J. Lavrin (London 1943), by J. Powys (London 1947), by A. Gide (N.Y. 1923, 1949).

The best translations of Tolstoy's works are in the Centenary Edition in twenty-one volumes by L. and A. Maude (London 1928–37), many of which have been included in the World's Classics series (London). Among numerous books on Tolstoy see *The Life of Tolstoy* in two volumes by A. Maude (London 1929-30), and *Leo Tolstoy* by E. Simmons (Boston 1946), a biography which contains a comprehensive bibliography. Also *Tolstoy in English*, a bibliographical study by A. Yassukovitch (N.Y. 1929). Tolstoy's philosophy of history is brilliantly analysed in *The Fox and the Hedgehog* by I. Berlin (London 1954). See also works by J. Lavrin (London 1944), L. Derrick (London 1944), and H. Faussett (London 1927).

For Leskov, see *The Cathedral Folk* translated by I. Hapgood (London 1924); *Tales* translated by N. Norman (London 1944); *The Enchanted Pilgrim* and *The Amazon* and other stories translated by D. Magarshack (London 1946 and 1949).

Chekhov's collected works translated by C. Garnett have been published in thirteen volumes (London 1916-22). See also his *Letters* translated by S. Koteliansky and R. Tomlinson (London 1925) and collections of stories not included in Garnett's edition: *The Woman in the Case* and other stories translated by A. Fitzlyon and K. Zinovieff (London 1953) and *The Unknown Chekhov* translated by A. Yarmolinsky (N.Y. 1954). The best translation of Chekhov's plays is by Stark Young; see his analysis of other versions in *The Sea Gull* (N.Y. 1939). See also M. Fell translations of the plays (N.Y. 1930). D. Magarshack's *Chekhov: A Life* is the most complete biography of the writer. *Chekhov* by R. Hingley (London 1950) contains a good bibliography. See also *Chekhov in English* by A. Heifetz (N.Y. 1948).

For the translations of the Decadents and Symbolists, see collections by Bowra, Yarmolinsky, Reavey, and Slonim. *The Little Demon* by F. Sologub is translated by J. Cournos and R. Aldington (N.Y. 1916). Merezhkovsky's *The Death of the Gods, The Romance of Leonardo da Vinci*, and *Peter and Alexis* translated by B. Guerney (N.Y. 1928–31). *Solovyov Anthology* edited by S. Frank (N.Y. 1950) has a bibliography of the English translations. *In Job's Balance* by L. Shestov was translated in 1932 (London). Berdiaev's *The Meaning of History, Spirit and Reality, The Russian Idea*, and others are available in English translations (London 1930, 1931, 1945).

Among the various collections of Gorky's tales *Gorky's Best Short Stories* translated by A. Yarmolinsky and M. Budberg (N.Y. 1939) is recommended. Gorky's three autobiographical novels—*Childhood, In the World*, and *My Universities*—have been published in one volume, *Autobiography of Maxim Gorky* translated by I. Schneider (N.Y. 1949); this is the only unabridged version. See also *Mother* translated by I. Schneider (N.Y. 1947), *The Artamonov Business* translated by A. Brown (London 1948), *The Life of Klim Samgin* (N.Y. 1930–8) of which *The Bystander* translated by B. Guerney, and *The Magnet, Other Fires*, and *The Spectre* translated by A. Bakshy. The latter also translated *Seven Plays by Gorky* (New Haven 1937). *Reminiscences* were translated by C. Mansfield, L. Woolf, and S. Koteliansky (London 1949). A survey of Gorky's life and work is in *Maxim Gorky and His Russia* by A. Kaun (N.Y. 1932). See also *From Pushkin to Mayakovsky* by J. Lavrin (London 1947).

Andreyev's *The Life of Man* translated by L. Meader and F. Scott (N.Y. 1915) and *He Who Gets Slapped* translated by G. Zilboorg (N.Y. 1922) are reprinted in various anthologies of drama. Other plays were published between 1915 and 1923. For his tales, see *The Seven Who Were Hanged* translated by H. Bernstein (N.Y. 1918) and *When the King Loses His Head* and other stories (London 1920). The most complete study of Andreyev is the book by A. Kaun (N.Y. 1935) with bibliography.

Bunin's best short stories are in three collections: *The Dreams of Chang, The Gentleman from San Francisco,* and *The Elaghin Affair* translated by B. Guerney (N.Y. 1923, 1934, 1935). See also *Dark Avenues* translated by R. Hare (London 1949) and the novels: *The Village* translated by I. Hapgood (London 1923), *The Well of Days* translated by G. Struve and H. Miles (N.Y. 1934). The 1926 edition of *Mitya's Love* is a poor re-translation from a French version.

Kuprin's tales are in *The River of Life* translated by S. Koteliansky and M. Murry (London 1916), *The Bracelet of Garnets* translated by L. Pasvolsky (N.Y. 1917), *Gambrinus* translated by Guerney (N.Y. 1925); see also his novels *The Duel* (London 1916) and *Yama the Pit* translated by B. Guerney (N.Y. 1930).

Poems of Blok are in anthologies by Bowra, Yarmolinsky, and Reavey and Slonim; *The Twelve* is translated by C. Bechhofer (London 1920) and also by B. Deutsch and A. Yarmolinsky (N.Y. 1931). For Mayakovsky, see *Mayakovsky and His Poetry* by H. Marshall (London 1945). For Pasternak—*The Collected Prose Works* translated by R. Payne and B. Scott (London 1945) and *Selected Poems* translated by J. Cohen (London 1947).

Only a few works by Remizov are available in English: *The Clock* translated by J. Cournos (London 1924), *The Fifth Pestilence* translated by A. Brown (London 1927), *On a Field Azure* translated by B. Scott (London 1946). The same applies to Prishvin: *Fen Cheng* translated by G. Walton and P. Gibbons (London 1936) and *The Lake and the Woods* translated by W. Goodman (London 1951).

The only translated work by Zamiatine is *We* translated by G. Zilboorg (N.Y. 1924).

Babel's *Collected Stories* by W. Morison were published in 1955 (N.Y.).

Most of the leading Soviet writers have been translated into English. For the bibliography of their works see *Soviet Russian Literature* by G. Struve (Norman 1951), *An Outline of Modern Russian Literature* by E. Simmons (N.Y. 1943), and bibliographical notes in *Modern Russian Literature* by M. Slonim (N.Y. 1953).

INDEX

171

Other SIGNET Books You Will Enjoy

MOBY DICK by Herman Melville

The sea epic of one-legged Captain Ahab and his crew who sailed out to battle the great white whale.

(#D1229—50¢)

THE WILD PALMS AND THE OLD MAN
by William Faulkner

Two novels about men and women in conflict with themselves and their surroundings. (#D1643—50¢)

APPOINTMENT IN SAMARRA by John O'Hara

Three days in the life of a man destroyed by his inability to cope with his personality. (#S1437—35¢)

TOBACCO ROAD by Erskine Caldwell

The robust bestseller of primitive living and loving in the rural South. (#S627—35¢)

DESIRE UNDER THE ELMS by Eugene O'Neill

This tragedy of a young girl's marriage to an elderly farmer is one of the greatest plays by the Nobel Prize winner. (#S1502—35¢)

BREAD AND WINE by Ignazio Silone

This compelling novel of Italy under fascism has humor, tragedy, compassion, and wisdom. (#D1545—50¢)

SONS AND LOVERS by D. H. Lawrence

The famous story of a son's efforts to find freedom from the consuming devotion of a possessive mother.

(#D1509—50¢)